Rubbing Shoulders

A MEMOIR

Rubbing Shoulders

A MEMOIR

by

Linda Hansen

Praise for Rubbing Shoulders

"Linda has touched me with *Rubbing Shoulders*. This story brings back life's greatest moments "

—George Noory,
host of *Coast to Coast Am* national radio

"As these pages reveal, Linda Hansen has worked with, and therefore 'rubbed shoulders' with, an impressive list of interesting, accomplished, and renowned people. Here's what she is too modest to say: We all kept asking for her because she was not only very good at what she did, but very good company as well."

—Bob Costas,
Legendary Emmy-Winning Sportscaster
& Baseball Hall of Famer

Linda Hansen takes us down memory lane with her memoir, *Rubbing Shoulders*. Born and raised in St. Louis, Missouri, this humble woman shares some of the remarkable opportunities that came her way in life. With dreams larger than the borders of University City could hold; not one to easily say no, Linda said yes to every chance she had to meet new people. From studying theater in New York to working as a makeup artist for celebrities, politicians, and sports stars, she was in the best possible position to meet many of the big names. Some of these people left lasting impressions and even became good friends. Join Linda as she shares a small piece of her life with us, inspiring us all to be more open to opportunity.

Rubbing Shoulders is the perfect title for this memoir, because that is exactly what the author did. Linda Hansen is intuitive when it comes to people, and it shows in her writing as well as her interactions with various celebrities. The majority of the experiences that she shares with us take place during the time frame of 1950 to 1980. She gives us her purest, most honest opinions on these encounters while also respecting the memory. What I love most about this book is that not for one moment did the author doubt her own ability or question whether she could do something. I respect her bravery in exploring the world, and I salute the love with which she has done it.

—5-star *Readers Favorite* review
Reviewed by Ronél Steyn for *Readers' Favorite*

Rubbing Shoulders
Copyright ©2025 by Linda Hansen

All rights reserved. No part of this book may be reproduced,
stored in a retrieval system, or transmitted in any form or by any means
— electronic, mechanical, photocopying, recording, or otherwise —
without the prior written permission of the author,
except for brief quotations in critical reviews or articles.

This is a work of nonfiction.
Except where noted, names, characters, places,
and incidents are a product of the author's memory and interpretation.

ISBNs:
Paperback 978-1-7378308-9-4
Ebook: 979-8-9935797-0-2
Audio 979-8-9935797-1-9

Library of Congress Control Number: 2025920253

Editor: Anne C. Jacob, Popin Edits
Cover Design: Richelle Jarc
Interior design and formatting: Nancy R. Koucky, NRK Designs
Photographs are from the personal collection of the author.

Requests for permission to reproduce material from this book,
and for publicity and author appearances contact:
www.lindahansenauthor.com/contact

Printed in USA
Publisher: Linda Hansen, Florida

Other works by Linda Hansen

Otto the Otter: A Big Surprise

and

Little Lost Dog, Looking for His Home

Preface

Perhaps you are not familiar with the term *rubbing shoulders*. It means associating or spending time with someone, especially someone important or famous. As you read my story, you will see that I have been fortunate to *rub shoulders* with many people. You may not know all the people whom I write about, but I suggest that you look them up. When you see a name in a **bold font**, it is someone with whom I did *rub shoulders*. Otherwise, the famous names are just that . . . famous people. At one time or another, all these people were well known.

Sharing only some of my personal life was a choice I made to help better explain who, what, where, and how my life evolved. This is not meant to be an autobiography in the traditional sense of the word. You will notice that the story is not always in chronological order. It is the story of moments in my life that were different from the experiences of many. I hope you will enjoy taking this journey with me.

Part I

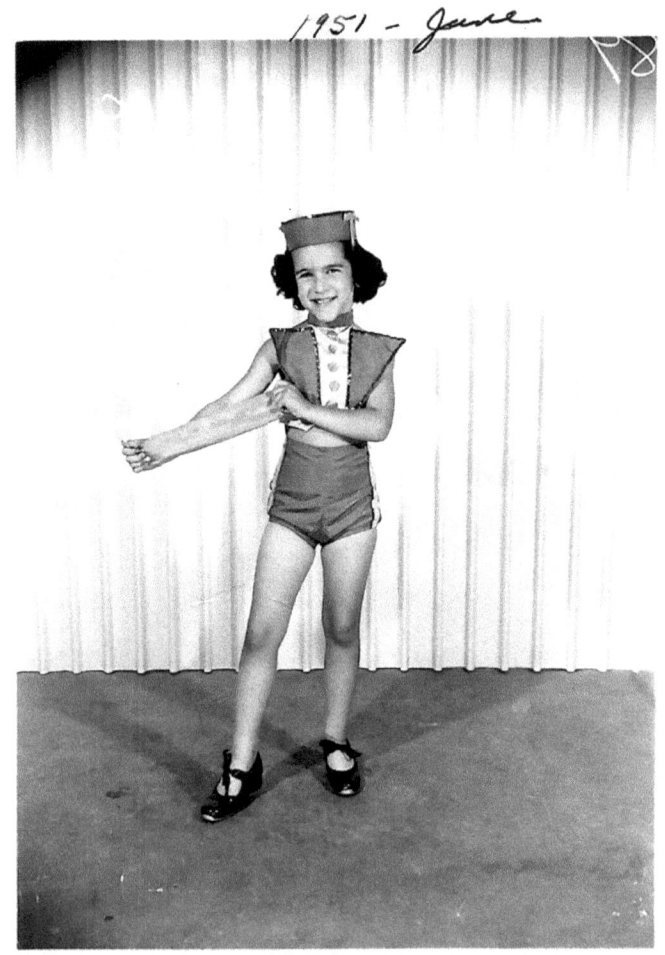

The author, dancing to the Chattanooga Shoeshine Boy, *1951*

Starting Out

You're from where? I am from University City. Many people don't know the name University City; it is a suburb of St. Louis. Although it is not truly a small town, as it has a population of about 35,000, it is a smaller city, and I think of myself as just a small-town girl.

My father bought a small, two-bedroom, one-and-a-half bath, all-brick home with a one-car garage in 1946 after his discharge from the Air Force and WWII. My parents moved into this home with their two-year-old daughter. I lived in this modest (not that I knew that) home until I was seventeen, when I left home to go to school in New York City and be on my own. Yes, I was adventurous . . . always was, and still am.

Looking back in time, I loved our home, and as a child growing up, I never knew whether we had or didn't have money. Of course, I don't think children think about money in the same manner as adults. We never needed anything, and I was not a spoiled child. Life was simple and good. Times were different then. There was no TV, telephones had party lines, and most homes did not have central air conditioning. We rarely ate out, not because we didn't have enough money; it was something we did for special occasions.

My memory is clear about the first time we ate at a pizza restaurant, and I know exactly where it was. Watching the men throw the pizza dough in the air was fascinating and something I had never seen before. As a teenager, I ate with my family at a Chinese restaurant for the first time, and I know what street it was on. The one place we ate at with regularity was a cafeteria in downtown St. Louis called Miss Hulling's. My father worked for his father in a family-owned business. My parents had only one car, and my grandfather drove my dad to work on Saturday mornings so my mother could have the car. We drove down to the store on Saturday afternoons, and when my dad shut and locked the door at the end of business, we would go have dinner on our way home.

It was not until forty-plus years later that I discovered that we didn't live in the better part of town. We did not live in the bad part of town, but we did not live in the better part of town. In my fifties, I was selling real estate and working with a young couple. The husband was a police officer in University City, and he needed to live there, not one of the other suburbs of St. Louis County. The couple decided to work with me because of my knowledge of the area. Ironically, they lived only a few blocks from my childhood home, where I had grown up. He told me the parameters of where he was willing to live, and when I asked him why he wouldn't accept a home in the area where he currently lived, he explained that it was not a good area. He told me it had never been as good as some of the other areas of University City.

As a child, I hadn't realized any of this and only became aware of class structure when I attended junior high school. It didn't have much of an impact on me, but I started to understand there were students who had attended other elementary schools that were different from those I had known for the prior six years of elementary school. Yes, I met some snobs, and no, they were not welcoming or friendly. What I knew was I didn't like them, and I didn't want to be like them.

Now, to the core of my story. Somehow, around age five, I knew I wanted to be a movie star. I do not remember exactly how it started, but I knew what I wanted to do when I grew up. As I have explained, we were not rich. However, my mother took me to the Carmen Thomas Dance Studio for tap dance lessons on the second floor of a building on Delmar Blvd., near DeBaliviere, in the city of St. Louis. We performed the Chattanooga Shoeshine Boy for our recital, and I thought we had the cutest costumes ever made. Mine is still in a trunk, and I cannot believe I was ever that tiny. We did another dance, like an Arabian Night, which I never liked as much, but this costume is also in the trunk. I took dance lessons there for only that one year. Looking back at these memories from a different vantage point, I understand this was probably a financial burden for my parents. In addition, my mother didn't drive at the time, and as a one-car family, my mother took me on a streetcar and bus to get to the classes!

Dancing lessons were followed by Junior Theater, which was in University City on the corner of Delmar and Hanley. The building is still there, and has been through many reincarnations; most recently, it was a dry cleaner. I was six years old, and my cousin, Howard, went with me (I think). During the fall, we were taught several poems to recite; one was about Frosty the Snowman—don't ask me the words, but I do remember that poor Frosty melted. The principal at Pershing Grade School, the elementary school I attended, was Mr. Ilgren. One of the most fantastic days in the life of this six-year-old first-grader was when Mr. Ilgren came to Miss Farmer, my teacher, and asked if he could take me out of class. He took me to the Parent Teacher's Organization (PTO), which was having a meeting (women/mothers only), introduced me to all these women, and had me recite my poem. Well, if there ever was a doubt, I knew for sure right then and there that this was the life for me.

The other thing that stands out in my mind from Junior Theater is that we performed *A Midsummer Night's Dream*. I was disappointed that I had one of those small, unimportant parts, but finally, the day came when it was time for the performance. I was devastated that several days before the show, I came down with chicken pox! I was so terrified and upset that I would not get to participate in the production. Fortunately, I got better and was able to be in the performance. I did not go back for another year. Again, in retrospect, this had to have been a financial burden for my parents, but they were doing their best to meet the desires of their spirited child.

As I explained, I never thought about how much money we had or what the cost of things was; what child does, but it did not stop me from wanting things. When I was eight, my parents surprised me and gave me a used, upright piano for my birthday. The wood on the piano had been painted a light green. It was not the most beautiful piano in the world, but to me it was. My parents gave me piano lessons, but sadly, the teacher did not teach me theory. She did teach me to sight-read, which I can still do to this day. The following years brought a variety of music teachers, none of whom were outstanding. Like most children, I did not practice enough, and none of them could truly motivate me. I would not have been a great talent, but this, coupled with the fact that none of them taught me theory and my lack of practice, well, you know the rest of the story. The good thing that came out of it is, all these years later, I still remember how to read music and can pound out a few notes when I need/want/can. I was given piano lessons again as a pre-teen, but this, too, was to no avail. It is a long story and does not truly relate to my journey.

My grandparents introduced me to theater, and I don't think they ever comprehended what they did. St. Louis is the home of The Muny, the St. Louis Municipal Theater, which is the oldest and largest outdoor musical theater in the United States. My grandparents had season tickets and started taking me with them when I was six years old. Every Wednesday, from the end of June until the beginning of August, they would pick me up at my home, after dinner, on their way to The Muny. I was small and could sit between their seats, and there was no charge to take me with them. As the years went by and I could no longer sit between their seats, I didn't go every week, but they took me to the shows I wanted to see. In the 1950s, the stars of shows that had been on Broadway traveled in the summer to perform at summer stock theaters, and The Muny was an important theater of its kind. I saw many well-known people perform there; the list would be overwhelming and far too many to try to name. My grandparents' seats were exactly center-stage, not in the orchestra section, but eight rows back from there. After they died, my mother kept these seats, and eventually I had the seats until I moved from St. Louis to Florida. I attended The Muny for sixty-five years!

Around the time I was ten or eleven, I had my first *Rubbing Shoulders* encounter. We had gone to Florida for vacation and went to what was then the renowned Cypress Gardens. **Bud Collyer**, best known for his work as the first host of the TV game shows *Beat the Clock* and *To Tell the Truth*, was filming a show there. I may have been young, but I was already very precocious and somehow thought I was sexy. Go figure! Anyway, for some reason, he spotted me, and I had my picture taken with him. Oh, I thought I was something!

The author, age ten or eleven, with Bud Collyer

Linda Hansen

Las Vegas Ad for Ray Bolger at the Sahara

My second *rubbing shoulders* moment happened in the summer of 1957, when I turned thirteen. My father took his first two-week vacation, and for my birthday present, my parents took me by car from St. Louis to California and back. They left my younger sister with my aunt and uncle, and we had an amazing vacation. We rode donkeys at Pikes Peak in Colorado, toured Salt Lake City, went fishing in Yellowstone National Park, rode the trolley in San Francisco, and went horseback riding in Yosemite National Park. In Los Angeles, we visited family and went to Disneyland, which had only been open for two years! Then we drove to Las Vegas. My parents got tickets for us to go see **Ray Bolger**. In case you don't recognize his name, he was an actor, singer, dancer, and stage performer, and is best remembered for his role as the Scarecrow in *The Wizard of Oz*. I was thrilled to go see him, and as we walked in, the maître d' spoke with my dad and told him they were putting us at a table right next to the stage, and that Mr. Bolger was going to incorporate my dad into his show. Was I excited? At one point during the show, Mr. Bolger was dancing and then "tripped" off the stage onto my dad's lap. He then invited my dad onto the stage, talked to him, and "apologized" for falling on him. When the show was over, our server asked us to wait as Mr. Bolger wanted to come out to meet us. This made my entire birthday trip even more special. He autographed a postcard the hotel had made for his show.

My desire to perform while I was in high school continued to grow. Several things happened there that helped motivate me. Singing and dancing were always important to me. University City High School had a great music teacher in Dr. Charles Procasky—Dr. Pro. I auditioned for Dr. Pro's a cappella choir and was accepted. We would rehearse, and I loved being part of all this. Two experiences, which as a teenager I thought were tragedies, made me drop out of what I was doing with Dr. Pro. In the scope of life, the use of the word tragedy is a little overblown, but I can tend to be melodramatic. Remember, I wanted to be an actress! The school had a jazz band, and they were holding auditions for singers to perform with the band. I made it to the finals and was so excited! I no longer remember why we did not have school on the day of the final audition, as it was a school day, but my mother got me to the audition late. I was mortified, as I knew getting there late was not acceptable, and it would jeopardize my opportunity of getting this incredible chance. Well, I was devastated. After she let me off at the front of the school, I went in, walked up the stairs, heard them already working, and I quietly went back down the stairs and walked the several miles back home, crying all the way. Sadly, this terrible day in the life of a fifteen-year-old only got worse. When I walked into our home crying, my mother told me that I was a selfish, self-centered child, as my grandfather had died that morning.

Linda Hansen

I continued to sing in the choir until that Christmas, when my dad forbade me from going caroling with the choir, as we were Jewish, and he refused to allow me to participate. Do you think there were a few fights in our home over this issue? After this, I just became too embarrassed to participate in anything with Dr. Pro. Oh, I forgot to say there was an entire group of us that had crushes on him. I have often thought about the fact that he was single, and while I don't know this for a fact, I am fairly sure he was gay. Remember, this was 1959–62, and life was much different than it is today. I look back on those years now and can think of several teachers I had in grade school and through high school who were probably homosexual. I am glad that times have changed. How terrible it must have been for these people to live in a closet.

For me, the best part of high school was the fact that, starting in the second semester of the sophomore year, girls were not required to take physical education, which I always hated and in which I never excelled. I jumped at the chance to take modern dance with Dena Madole, who was the next teacher to have an impact on my life. I learned modern dance with this gifted teacher and had class with her every day. There was an after-school dance club, Taberna, of which I became a member and later president. In my senior year, I was able to have dance classes twice a day, every day, as the school had added a new class, choreography, which we could take. Miss Madole gave me the opportunity to choreograph a major piece for a concert that our high school symphony gave in the spring of my senior year. Miss Madole believed in my skill and helped me believe in myself.

People often talk about the teacher they had who had the biggest impact on their lives. I was most fortunate to have Amy Neukomm as my sixth-grade teacher. Miss Neukomm was a wonderful woman who saw all the abilities that were tucked away inside of me. She motivated me to be a good student, if only for this one year. She was the teacher who changed my life and is what all teachers should be so fortunate to achieve in their careers. We all had autograph books for the end of the school year and the end of our grade school years. Miss Neukomm told us if we would give her enough time to keep our autograph book, that she would write us a poem.

> *A young girl named Linda, tis true*
> *Talks more than a girl should do*
> *But she is gay and she's witty*
> *Pleasant and pretty*
> *Her friends will never be few.*

Hard to believe the impact these words had on me and that I remember them so vividly all these years later. Miss Neukomm urged me to follow my dreams. And, she was so correct . . . I did and still do "talk more than a girl should do." Miss Neukomm remained part of my life even after I moved to New York. She, too, loved the theater and had saved all the playbills from the shows she had seen. As she aged, she gave them to me. Sadly, I no longer have them. When I was sixteen, I was cast as the geisha girl in *The Teahouse of the August Moon* in a production by a very well-respected amateur/community theatrical group, The Southtown Players. While I didn't have any English to speak in the play, I was the female lead. I was excited beyond words to have been cast in this part after open auditions. Miss Neukomm came to see me perform, and as a gift, she brought me a pair of silver and turquoise earrings in the shape of a horseshoe for good luck. I don't wear them, but I still have them and keep them with all my other jewelry.

I was fortunate to continue working with The Southtown Players throughout my high school years. They were the first amateur theater in the United States to produce *The Miracle Worker*, and I was overwhelmed

Linda Hansen

when, at seventeen, I was cast in the role of Annie Sullivan. Shortly after the cast announcements were made, I received notice that I had been accepted into one of the theater schools in New York City, to which I had applied, and I would not be in St. Louis for the scheduled performances. I was so disappointed. I called the director, and we had lunch together. She said I shouldn't even think twice about having to turn the role down and that I should go to the school for which I auditioned.

The author performing in
The Teahouse of the August Moon

Part II

Concerts in My Teens

My parents had no interest in jazz. I think most of the time, they did not understand where, why, or how they became saddled with this teenager who was so different and marched to a different drummer. This was an attitude that never changed. I know my parents loved me, but to them I was different . . . At least that is how I perceived it then and still perceive it today.

At some point during middle school, when people were discovering rock 'n' roll, I discovered jazz. I no longer remember what drew me to this music; it may have been my subconscious desire to always be different, but I discovered an interest in jazz that would last the rest of my life. There was a disc jockey on the 'black' radio station, KATZ, named Spider Burks. He hosted a show called *Jazz on Sunday Afternoon*, and I listened to it faithfully every week. While other kids my age were discovering Elvis Presley, who I never liked, I was listening to Miles Davis, Cannonball Adderley, John Coltrane, Count Basie, Ella Fitzgerald, and the other jazz greats of the day. I am sure part of my passion for jazz extended from my desire to be in show business. Not only did I wish to act, but I wanted to sing . . . to be a singer in the mode of Billie Holiday, Lena Horne, Peggy Lee, and the other great female vocalists of the day.

In the late 1950s through the 1960s, St. Louis had an active entertainment area called Gas Light Square. There were several blocks of restaurants, nightclubs, bars, and a theater. I was too young to be able to take much advantage of the benefits Gas Light Square provided, as I was in high school and unable to enter the bars to listen to the entertainment, but there were two coffeehouses. The *Laughing Buddha* was one of them, and it featured folk singers. The other, *Jorgie's*, featured jazz, and since this was my passion, this is the place where I hung out. I was sixteen, had my driver's license, and would be there almost every week. Depending on who was performing, I could be there three to five nights a week! My mother always knew where I was, and I knew what time I had to be home. I had time to be there for one set during the week and at least two sets on the weekend. If my mother needed to speak with me for some reason, she would call me there, and they would come to get me to use their phone. I was a groupie before the word existed. The owner, Jorge Martinez, always greeted me and, depending on who the performer was, would introduce me to them. I had the opportunity to meet some of the jazz greats of the time, such as **Wes Montgomery**, **Lou Donaldson**, and **Horace Silver**. There was a time that I had autographed albums for each of them, but sadly, the albums are long gone. Jorge would bring these jazz greats to my table in between sets, and they would kindly sit with this teenager who was filled with such passion for what they did.

During these years, jazz concerts would come to town and be performed at the Kiel Opera House and Kiel Auditorium. I was fortunate to have an uncle, Uncle Frank, who loved jazz and loved me. My uncle would get tickets for the concerts that I really wanted to see, and he, my Aunt Dorothy, and I would go to see the performers that captured my attention.

ELLA FITZGERALD

One of these concerts was by the great legend, **Ella Fitzgerald**. Uncle Frank always bought good seats, usually in the center of the orchestra. He was a primary care physician, and in those days, was the kind of doctor who was always on call. I remember he would give his pager to an usher and make sure the usher knew where he was sitting in case the exchange called and needed him. This was in the late 1950s and early 1960s, and the concept of cell phones would have been science fiction. Uncle Frank was known to take advantage of the fact that he was a doctor. He knew how to get things. During the intermission on the night we went to see Ella Fitzgerald, he told Aunt Dorothy and me that he didn't think Miss Fitzgerald felt well. He could tell the way she was performing and using her handkerchief to wipe her face. During intermission, he went backstage to offer his services to her. Hard to believe, but when he returned to his seat, yes, she was not feeling well and was eager and very happy to have been able to see a doctor. He went to his car to get his black bag so he could look at her throat, etc. She kindly told him to come back after the show and to bring his family with him. The show ended, and the three of us went backstage. Much to my excitement, we were taken to her dressing room. We sat and chatted with this lovely and gracious woman. As the time came to leave, she asked if we knew where a nightclub called "Davey 'Nose' Bold's" was. She said a friend of hers was performing there and had asked her to come by after her show. She wanted to know if it was far away and if she would be able to take a taxi there. My uncle explained that taking a taxi there would be unsafe for her, as, sadly, St. Louis was not a very integrated city and that it would not be the safest thing for her to do. Uncle Frank explained to her that it was not far and that we would drive past it on our way home. He asked if she would like a ride there, and much to my shock and excitement, she said, "Yes!" Uncle Frank went to get the car while Aunt Dorothy and I stayed with Ella until he returned to the stage door to pick us up. I sat in the back seat with her until we got to the club. She got out of the car and thanked Uncle Frank for the ride. I could not believe what had happened. Unfortunately, as it was a nightclub that served alcohol, we could not go in because of me. I would have loved to have been able to go, as her friend who was performing was Mel Torme!

Linda Hansen

CARLOS MONTOYA

Besides my interest in jazz, I was fascinated with flamenco guitar, which is very similar to jazz, as they both focus on rhythm and improvisation. The great **Carlos Montoya** came to perform at the Kiel, and by now, I had learned it was easy to get backstage and meet the headliner. Of course, this opportunity has greatly changed over the years, and it has become very difficult to meet a performer. This was the spring of 1962. I was allowed into his dressing room after the show and met Mr. Montoya and his wife. We spent some time talking about his music, about the poor Spanish I spoke, and the fact that I had been admitted to the Neighborhood Playhouse School of the Theater in New York City and would be moving there in August of that year. It is hard to believe, in this day and age, but the Montoyas gave me their phone number and told me to call once I was in New York. I called them that October, and they invited me to their apartment for a visit. I took a taxi over to their apartment, met their son, spent a delightful evening with them, and never saw them again. I have no memory as to why I didn't see them again, but as I look back at some of these brief encounters, I think that, although I was brave, even brazen in certain ways, I did not have the social skills or knowledge to know how to continue these relationships. I always thought I had nothing to bring to the table, and would not follow through with seeing people again. How naïve of me. It definitely shows my lack of maturity and knowledge. I wonder now what I could have done with all the opportunities I let pass me by.

SONNY PAYNE

On another one of my excursions to a concert at the Kiel Opera House with Uncle Frank and Aunt Dorothy, we saw the great Count Basie Orchestra. The Count Basie Orchestra was a sixteen- to eighteen-piece big band and was one of the most prominent jazz performing groups from the 1930s through the 1960s. This night, I became enthralled with the flashy drummer, **Sonny Payne**. Sonny Payne was a jazz drummer, best known

Rubbing Shoulders

for his work with Count Basie, and later was the drummer that Frank Sinatra would want to play for him whenever he appeared with the Count Basie band. As usual, after the concert, Uncle Frank asked if I would like to go meet the drummer. Uncle Frank was never shy about introducing himself to people. So, backstage we went, and the next thing I knew, we were talking to the drummer, Sonny Payne. He was friendly and spent time speaking with his fan. He gave me one of the sets of sticks he had used that night, and I went home thinking I was really something. The sticks were all marked and scuffed from his using them to hit the rims of the drums, but to me, they were a treasure.

For some reason, I gave him my phone number, and in retrospect, I have wondered why, but every few months, he would call my home and talk to me. This was around 1960, when the world was still segregated. As I look back on it, I question his motivation. I was a white teenager, and he was a black jazz musician. He would call from the road and call when he was in St. Louis for another performance. This relationship went on for several years. Eventually, I knew I was going to be living in New York City, and while speaking with him one time, I told him I would be moving there. Sonny said I should pay attention to the shows at Basin Street East, a notable nightclub of the 1960s in New York City, as the band often played there, and he would make the arrangements necessary for me to come see them play.

Starting in September 1962, I was eighteen years old and living in New York City in an apartment on 88th St. and York Ave. with my roommate, Lindy, who was a classmate of mine at the Neighborhood Playhouse School of the Theater. Eventually, I saw the Basie Band was going to be at Basin Street East, called Sonny, and he made arrangements for me to attend the show. During that year, I was at Basin Street almost every night the band was in town. Most of the time I went alone, but there were times I took other classmates with me. Sonny always made sure there was a table reserved in my name, and he would come and sit with me, and whoever was with me, between sets. Everyone knew I was the band mascot . . .

who knew the word "groupie" in those days? Even the Count knew who I was. If he walked by my table, he never spoke with me, but he would grunt at me as his way of acknowledging me and saying hi.

After the show, Sonny would take me with him wherever he was going. One night, we went to Jilly's, a famous nightclub of the time, and met with Louis Prima, Keely Smith, and some of his other friends. On another night, he dropped me off at Birdland. Originally opened in 1949 and located on Broadway and 52nd St, it was a hotbed of jazz. Sonny left me and two of my friends there so we could go see Gerry Mulligan, who was primarily known as one of the leading jazz baritone saxophonists of the time. Sonny did not go with us as he had other plans. Pee Wee Marquette was famous as the bouncer at Birdland, and Sonny told him we had to leave at 3 a.m., no matter what. In the middle of a set, Pee Wee came to our table, leaned over to me, and said we had to leave. I said, "No, I don't want to leave in the middle of the set," and he replied that Sonny had just called to check on us and that we had to leave . . . end of story . . . no further discussion. Unhappily, we left.

Another night, after the band's performance at Basin Street, I got into Sonny's car. I no longer remember where we were going, but sitting next to me in the front seat was **Nipsy Russell**, a comedian who was also known for his appearances on TV. In the back seat were three members of the band, including the trombone player, **Grover Cleveland**. Thinking back to those times, these guys were really pushing the envelope. Here I was, an eighteen-year-old white girl in a car with five black jazz musicians and entertainers! And, they were smoking pot! Nipsy had the joint and attempted to pass it to me. Sonny, who was driving, reached across me, hit Nipsy, and said, "Don't be givin' that s**t to her!" So, the joint went right past me and into Sonny's hand. The guys all smoked, but no one gave me the opportunity again. They did understand, even if I did not. Only one more memory of these evenings with Sonny stands out, and it is of an evening when we went to someone's apartment on the Upper West Side.

When we got to the apartment where everyone was hanging out, the great **Joe Williams**, another well-known jazz singer, was there. I was thrilled to spend time talking to this icon of the jazz world. As usual, 3 a.m. was my bewitching hour, and Sonny would either drive me home from wherever we were or he would hail me a taxi to make sure I was taken home. I can't tell you why my time as the Basie Band groupie came to an end, but it did. It lasted only for that one year.

JOEL GREY

During the 1950s and 60s, traveling Broadway shows would be at the American Theater, which no longer exists, in St. Louis. Although I didn't get to see every show, my mother would get tickets for the shows that I really wanted to see. I was home, after my first year at school in New York, for two weeks before I had to be in Stowe, VT, where I had a job doing summer stock as the resident ingenue. **Joel Grey** was performing in *Stop the World—I Want to Get Off*, and my mother took me to see the show. While reading the program, I noticed he was a graduate of the school I was attending, the Neighborhood Playhouse School of the Theater.

As you have already learned, I am not shy! After the show, I went backstage and asked to see Joel Grey. I was taken to his dressing room, introduced myself, and told him I was a student at the *Playhouse*. He could not have been nicer or more gracious. He spent quite some time chatting with me and asked what year student I was. I explained that I had just finished the first year, and he asked if I was going back for the second year. I said I did not know yet, as I was still waiting for the letter, as completion of the first year did not mean you were automatically accepted into the second year. The class would be cut by approximately 50 percent, so you went home and had to wait for the letter, which told you if you were going to be able to return. Mr. Grey smiled at me and said if I received my letter while he was in St. Louis to call him. Amazingly, two days later, my letter of acceptance arrived. I called him and told him the good news. He was almost as excited as I was, if that was possible.

Linda Hansen

SUMMER STOCK

I graduated from high school on a Friday in June 1962, and the next day took a Trailways bus to Boston. My mother had a dear high school friend who lived there with her husband and two sons. They picked me up at the bus station, and I spent the night with them. The next morning, they drove me to the Northshore Music Theater in Beverly, MA, where I had already been hired to be an apprentice for the summer. I was seventeen when I arrived and turned eighteen while I was working there.

As an apprentice, you are assigned to work, at one time or another, in every department from shop to costumes to lighting. It was an incredible experience, and I learned so much. The theater was a theater in the round and one of the most respected summer stock theaters in the country. It was a star system theater, which meant that each show had someone of renown starring. Often, as apprentices, we did not have too much interaction with the star. At other times, because of our specific job or because of who the individual person was, we did have the opportunity to work with the star.

When I arrived at the theater, they were doing a production of *The King and I*. I was assigned the job of being in the men's dressing room to help the performers put on Texas Dirt, which was the makeup product used to make their skin look darker and more like the Siamese they were portraying. I helped all the singers and dancers, but I was also assigned to work specifically with the star of the show, **Jose Duval**. Not many people knew him by his name, but people did know him as Juan Valdez, the Columbia Coffee Bean Man. Now remember, I was seventeen at the time. I was shocked the first night as I had never seen men running around in dance belts and/or their underwear. It was an education. It took me three nights to realize that Jose would bring a fifth of vodka into his dressing room every night, and by the end of the night, it would be gone. One night, he was quite drunk, and he injured one of the other performers. The next night, he came in and placed his bottle of vodka on the dressing table. I told him he could not have it. We got into a minor verbal disagreement, and I had the nerve to grab the bottle and empty it down the sink! I look back at it now and cannot believe I had that much nerve. Amazingly, after yelling at me, we became friends. On the last night, he gave me his phone number and said when I got to New York that I should call him. We saw each other a few times for meals after I moved to New York.

Gypsy Rose Lee was a burlesque entertainer famous for her striptease act, and an actress who came to the theater to star in Mame. I had no contact with her, but she was the first performer that I had been around who was totally out of control. She arrived at the theater with her two dogs. They were Crested Chinese, and at that time, no one had ever seen or heard of this breed. Her two dogs were very aggressive, and they bit one of the men who worked in the set department. She was told she could not bring the dogs to the theater again. She would storm around the theater, yelling and cussing at anyone in sight. An expert at throwing temper tantrums, on the night of dress rehearsal, she demanded that many of the sets be changed, causing them to still be wet on opening night, and the actors were not able to sit on many of the chairs. During the dress rehearsal, **Margaret Whiting**, who was a singer of popular music, was brought to the theater. She was to start rehearsals the next day for the show, *Gypsy*, which was a musical about the life of Gypsy Rose Lee. Ms. Whiting was going to be portraying the role of Gypsy Rose Lee's mother. As Ms. Whiting entered the theater, Ms. Lee was throwing yet another tantrum. I was standing near enough that I observed Ms. Whiting as she looked at the director and said, "I'm playing *her* mother!" It may have been one of the funniest lines I have ever heard.

Margaret Whiting was the opposite of Gypsy Rose Lee. She was kind and friendly and learned the names of every person who worked at the theater. She had her twelve-year-old daughter with her, and my job assignment was to help take care of her daughter. Margaret Whiting did two things that stand out in my mind all these years later. There is a scene in *Gypsy* where a song, "Have an Eggroll Mr. Goldstone," is sung, and

Chinese food is eaten. On the last night, when there was a wrap party, Margaret Whiting showed up and brought Chinese food for everyone. The other special thing she did was she bought me a small book as a thank you for all the help I had given to her and her daughter. I had the book until I retired and moved to Florida, when I didn't keep any of the books I owned—this also included my copy of *Gypsy*, the autobiographical memoir Gypsy Rose Lee wrote and sent to all the apprentices as a thank you.

Linda Lavin co-starred with Margaret Whiting in *Gypsy*. She played the role of Gypsy Rose Lee. At the time, she was twenty-five years old and had already made a dent in the musical theater scene in New York City. One of my jobs for the week was to be her dresser. As I explained, the Northshore Music Theater was a theater in the round. There was no backstage. Outside of certain exits, there were small, burlap dressing rooms. There was a very brief break between Linda/Gypsy making an exit from the stage and having a very quick clothing change. This was a major costume change that led to the scene where Gypsy performs her first strip, and Linda had to have five or six costumes placed one on top of the other so she could do her strip. We literally had only three minutes to get this done. Well, one night while getting her dressed I zipped her skin into one of the dresses. I could not get the zipper to move; we were running out of time, and Linda told me to just do it. Yes, I made her skin bleed, but I was able to get her skin out of the zipper and get her dressed. She was so professional, and she never said a word to me about it. Linda Lavin went on to a very successful career as an award-winning actress on TV in shows such as *Alice* and on Broadway.

The summer was filled with stories and excitement. I had the opportunity to work with so many people. Some were famous, some had been famous, and some were to become famous later. Two of the people who became famous later were **Doris Roberts** and **Alan Oppenheimer**. My eighteenth birthday was on a Wednesday, and amazingly it turned out that it was also my day off. Doris and Alan had made plans to go sailing for the day, and when they found out it was my birthday, they asked me to join them. I had never been on a sailboat before, and the opportunity to spend the day sailing out of Marblehead, MA, with these two wonderful and thoughtful actors was a highlight of the summer. They each went on to success. Doris became well known for her role in *Everybody Loves Raymond*, and Alan was in the *Six Million Dollar Man* and many other movies and TV shows.

The person who stands out in my mind as one of the all-time most obnoxious people with whom I have ever come in contact was **Victor Borge**. Victor Borge came to the theater for a one-night performance. He was rude and mean-spirited, and we were told not to speak to him. He did two things that became memorable to this impressionable teenager. During the intermission, he chose to stand in an area where the public could see him. I saw a young girl, approximately eight years old, ask, "Mr. Borge, may I have your autograph?" Without saying a word to her, he just turned his back on her and spoke with his assistant. As the show ended, his next action, to me, was indefensible. He came out the exit and said, "Get the lights up and get those fuckers out!" I was stunned, not by the language, but by the attitude. Without 'those fuckers' paying to come see him, he would not have made all the money he did as a performer. I have never met anyone else who had such disregard for the public.

One of the young men who worked in the set construction department at the theater was Dall Forsythe, the son of **John Forsythe**, known for his roles in movies and TV. For a week or so, Dall gave me a lot of attention and would go back with me to the home where I was staying for the summer. Remember, I was still seventeen at the time. Yes, we necked, but he wanted more, and as a virgin, I knew I was not ready to take this next step, so this was the end of our friendship. Many years later, I met his father, John Forsythe, but the rest of this story is yet to come.

As the summer went on, I got sick with what I thought was a cold. After a few days of not feeling well, I started to run a fever. Several days went by, and the fever became quite high, and I was unable to speak. The theater flew me home to St. Louis. I landed around 3 p.m. My parents picked me up and took me straight to the hospital, where I remained for a week, and it turned out that I had a very severe case of mononucleosis. I was terrified it was going to be a problem for me to get to New York to start my school, but fortunately, I got better, and the doctors told me I could leave and start my new life.

SUMMER STOCK PART 2

I did two seasons of summer stock, and the second season, the summer of 1963, was in Stowe, Vt. Stowe was, and is, famous as a skiing location, but it is beautiful in the summer and has a steady stream of tourists. There was an old barn that had been turned into a theater, and this is where I spent the summer, again working as an apprentice and the female ingénue. During the day, I oversaw the box office, and unless I was performing in a show, which was not every week, I was responsible for the box office in the evening as well.

I did perform in several shows with small parts, either as a walk-on or with a few lines, but in one show, I was the lead! The show was *The Chalk Garden*, about a troubled young girl. One night after a performance, I was in the dressing room taking off my makeup, when one of the other performers came into the dressing room and told me there was someone who wanted to speak with me. Me! I could not imagine who it might be. I quickly went out to speak with whomever it was. Much to my amazement, the person waiting to meet me was **Maria Von Trapp**. Yes, it was Maria Von Trapp of *The Sound of Music* fame. Their family had settled in Stowe, as it reminded them of home. They had opened a ski lodge, and the residents of Stowe knew the family lived there, but the family tended to keep to themselves. I did not know they lived there, and I was shocked that Mrs. Von Trapp wanted to meet with me. We sat and chatted for a while. She was kind, encouraging, and very complimentary to my acting abilities. She was very gracious, and I was incredibly surprised when she

Rubbing Shoulders

invited me to come visit the lodge if I had some time off. I explained that my parents were going to arrive in a few weeks and that I would be leaving with them. She thoughtfully said I should come up when they were in town. My parents arrived, and we went to the lodge that afternoon. I asked to see Mrs. Von Trapp. She came out of her office to greet us and then assigned someone to take us on a tour of the lodge.

Part Three

NEW YORK, NEW YORK

WHAT TOOK ME to New York City, and why did I want to go? My desire to be a performer never waned. I auditioned for the American Academy of Dramatic Arts and the Neighborhood Playhouse School of the Theater in my senior year of high school and was excited when I was accepted to attend both schools. I chose to enroll in the two-year program at the Neighborhood Playhouse. Over the years, many well-known and respected actors attended the school. Unfortunately, the director of the school, Sanford Meisner, took a sabbatical during this time, and it is interesting to note that none of the students who attended the school while he was gone became successful in a big way. Regardless, the two years I was there brought great education and opportunities my way.

Modern dance and movement were major parts of the curriculum. I was fortunate to train with **Bertram Ross** and **Bettie de Jong**, lead dancers with the world-renowned modern dance company of **Martha Graham**. Several times they urged me to audition to become a member of her company, but I knew in my heart that I did not have all the skills that were needed to be part of this prestigious dance company. One of the most exciting days was when Martha Graham came to teach one of our classes. The opportunity to spend a two-hour class under her instruction was almost more than this eighteen-year-old could stand. I was beside myself with excitement. Martha Graham was known for using many physical descriptions when she was teaching dance class. She wanted us to jump in a particular manner and said that we should jump from our vagina. She went up to one of my fellow classmates who wasn't jumping the way she, Ms. Graham, wanted. She shoved her finger up the girl's leotard and said, "This is your vagina." Needless to say, I was shocked.

In addition to modern dance classes, there was also a movement class that included choreography instruction. The teacher of this class was **Louis Horst.** He was a composer and had been a lover of Martha Graham's. His co-teacher in these classes was **Pearl Lang**, another well-known modern dancer of that period. Speaking of these famous dancers, to people who are not familiar with the dance world, their names will not mean anything, but the two years I trained with these people is filled with memories.

Louis Horst was seventy-nine years old when I met him and started to study with him. Early in one of our classes, he asked where I was from, and I told him St. Louis. He replied, "St. Louie." I corrected him and explained that people from St. Louis did not call it St. Louie. A sly grin appeared on his face as he asked me how I said his name, and I replied. "Louie." He asked how it was spelled, and I said, "L-O-U-I-S." He again gave me that sly smile and said, "That is why you come from St. Louie!" What he did not tell me was that he was born in Kansas City, MO, and knew exactly how to pronounce St. Louis. This started an unusual relationship with this great man until he died during my second year of study with him. Pearl Lang was not happy with the relationship I shared with Louis, but I became the teacher's pet. I was expected to sit on the floor next to where he sat, and he would talk with me throughout the class. During the second year, he became extremely ill, was hospitalized, and died in January of 1964. He was sent home from the hospital, and I was permitted to visit him at his apartment during the brief time before he died.

Paul Morrison became the director of the Neighborhood Playhouse in the fall of 1962. I was fortunate to develop a good relationship with Paul, who designed sets, lighting and/or costumes for such shows as *All*

Rubbing Shoulders

My Sons (1947), *Candide* (1956), *Much Ado About Nothing* (1959), and others. This was another time that someone of fame decided to take an interest in me. One day, Paul called me to his office and asked if I could wait at the front door for a special guest they were expecting. I said yes, and then he told me I was to be the escort for **Sammy Davis, Jr.!!!** I did everything I could to appear calm, as he was one of my very favorite performers. I waited for him, he arrived, I took him to the elevator, and then rode up with him as I took him to the room where he was to speak with the second-year students. Although he was at the school to speak with the students who were graduating that year, I was told I could stay and hear him speak. During the things he talked about, he said he had perfect pitch. I had never met anyone who said this and asked about it. He said I should come to the piano that was in the room and press on any note, while he had his back to me, and he would tell me what note I played. He had me do this for several different notes, and he was correct each time. He was polite to me, and this was definitely a moment of *rubbing shoulders*.

Paul Morrison continued to have me do other things as well. In the fall of 1963, the school became the venue for a performance of a show that was not on Broadway, but the play was being used as part of a workshop/showcase for the Actors Studio. The director was **Ed Sherin**, who was a TV and Broadway director. As Paul Morrison had already befriended me, he gave me opportunities that not everyone else had. Mr. Sherin needed a director's assistant, and Paul assigned me to work with him. My responsibility was to always be at his side, pad and pencil in hand, and take his comments down regarding staging, actors' performances, and any other detail. After rehearsal, the actors would gather on stage, and sitting next to him, I would tell him each of his notes, at which time he would relay this to the actors, make any changes, and so forth. This is what the rehearsal process is all about, and it was a tremendous opportunity for a nineteen-year-old theater student. The show starred a young **Billy Dee Williams,** and Billy and I became friends and hung out together for the six months of rehearsal. Billy went on to much success on Broadway, in

45

movies, and on TV. He became known for his iconic portrayal of Lando Calrissian in the original *Star Wars* trilogy, many TV shows, and he also had the leading role in the 1972 Billie Holiday biopic *Lady Sings the Blues*.

AL KASHA

Hard to remember the date, and I must admit that I do not remember how, but around the time I was twenty-one or twenty-two, I met and started to date **Al Kasha**. We dated for almost two years. Al was a hard-working composer who worked for Bob Crewe. Crewe was a well-known music/record producer at that time. Al and his partner, **Joel Hirschhorn**, wrote songs that would then be put onto the albums Crewe was producing. During this time, they did not have any big hits, but they were getting paid for writing music. At one point, Lesley Gore was cutting a new album, and she was singing one of their songs. Al took me to the recording studio the night they were recording the song he and Joel wrote. I was about twenty-three, and thought it was so exciting. At the time, it was my dream to be in the position where I was recording an album. It was the second time I had been in a big studio and had the experience of seeing how it was done. Al and Joel eventually went to Hollywood and won an Academy Award for the Best Song of the year for "The Morning After" from *The Poseidon Adventure*, and many other awards. He wrote songs and music for other movies, television series, and Broadway. I was long out of the picture by this time, married and back living in St. Louis, but it was certainly a time in my life when I was again *rubbing shoulders*.

FESTIVAL MOVIE THEATER

PETER, PAUL, AND MARY

I was fortunate to always be in unique positions, even when I did not realize that I was. When I was twenty years old, I got a job selling tickets at the Festival Movie Theater on 57th Street, just west of 5th Avenue. The theater was next to Henri Bendel, which was then and until it closed in

2019, an exclusive women's clothing store. The movie theater was half a block from Tiffany's, the Plaza Hotel was a block away, and because of the theater's proximity to these exclusive and upscale businesses, I often saw people coming in and out of Bendel's and walking on the street. The ticket booth at the Festival was a glass-enclosed, pentagon-shaped booth that sat out in front of the theater. I had a clear view of everyone who walked down 57th Street. I did not get to meet the people, but one person who clearly caught my attention as he walked by one evening was Salvador Dali. On another day, a presidential cavalcade with Lyndon B. Johnson drove by the theater, giving me a front-row seat.

There were many people who walked by regularly, and they would wave, smile, say hello, or acknowledge my presence in some way. One of the regular walkers was a man who walked by carrying his bass. He would often smile and say a few words to me. One night, he stopped and said they were recording in the building next to the movie theater, and if I wanted, I was welcome to come up when I finished work, which was around 11:30 p.m. to midnight. When I got off work, I walked next door, pushed the buzzer, and went up to the studio. I laugh at how naïve I was, again, and at how I didn't realize who many of the people that I met were. The bassist and composer was **Bill Lee**, who did session work as a first-call musician and band leader to many of the twentieth century's most significant musical artists. He was Spike Lee's father, who went on to much fame and success as an Academy Award-winning movie director. I sat and listened to two men and a woman record a song—Puff the Magic Dragon! It wasn't until it became a big hit that I realized I had been with Peter, Paul, and Mary and had not even known it.

GARY MERILL

During the time I worked at the Festival Movie Theater, **Gary Merill** came to the theater one night. He was waiting outside at the front of the theater for friends and decided to have a chat with me. It was not unusual for people to speak with me. It happened relatively often. I have always been an outgoing, gregarious, friendly soul who would talk to almost anyone. Remember, I was the eleven-year-old "who talked more than a child should do." I was still at work when Gary left the movie, and he stopped to talk with me again. While we talked, I said how much I loved going to the movies, and that one of the perks of my job was that I could get passes to go to any movie I wished. I do not know why, but he asked for my phone number, gave me his, and said, "Let's go to the movies sometime." This chance meeting developed into a friendship that lasted about one-and-a-half years. We would go to afternoon movies together, using the free passes I was able to get, and he would take me out to lunch before the movie or dinner afterwards. Gary lived in an apartment building on Central Park West, somewhere in the 80s or 90s. At times, he would call me and say, "Come over for dinner." He liked to cook, and we would sit and talk. Now, one of the most important things about Gary was that he had been the fourth husband of Bette Davis. She called on one of the nights when I was at his apartment. Sometimes he would take me to a party, and one evening stands out in my mind. Again, my naivety is apparent. The party was a fundraising event for SNCC. I did not know who or what they were! Little did I realize that the liberal-thinking performers of the time, including people such as Lee Grant, were at the party. It all went right over my head. I no longer remember who was at the party, but it was packed, wall to wall, with famous people.

 I was still only twenty years old. At the time, and coming from my modest family, there were many experiences I never had. On our first afternoon "go to the movies" date, Gary took me to a French restaurant. I had never been in a French restaurant, was overwhelmed by the menu, and didn't know what any of the strange foods were. When the waiter came to our table to take our order, I made sure I ordered something with which I was familiar. Gary looked at me and asked if I didn't want some escargot. Escargot!!! I didn't even know what it was, and since I was attempting to be something more than I was, I said no, that I didn't want any. Well, the escargot was brought out for Gary to eat, and I thought, oh, my heavens. He asked if I would like one or two, and I said no, that I wasn't a big eater and would have a difficult time eating my meal.

Several months later, my mother came to visit me, and we went to dinner with a family friend from our days in New Mexico who now lived in New York. We went to a French restaurant, and of course, escargot was on the menu. I asked if it was okay if I ordered it and explained that I had never had it and wanted to try it. I knew that if I didn't like it, then it would be okay if I didn't finish it. I loved it and have been eating escargot ever since.

SAMMY DAVIS—PART TWO

My second meeting with Sammy Davis was while I was at the Festival Movie Theater. Sammy Davis had rented the theater one evening, after the last show of the night, for a private party and a showing of the movie that was there at the time, for the cast and crew of his Broadway show, *Golden Boy*. Several of us were asked to stay and help with the concessions or anything else that might be needed. I cannot name any of the other people with him, but he was there with his wife, Mai Britt. I made no attempt to speak with him, and I knew he would never remember the eighteen-year-old who had been his escort at the Neighborhood Playhouse two years earlier, but it was exciting just to be in his presence and to be part of the energy that always surrounded him.

AL PACINO

It was common that many of the people who worked at movie theaters were starving actors. They were able to work at night so they could take classes and make rounds during the day. And, as I mentioned, a side benefit was the fact that we could get free passes to go to other movies. At the time, I was going on auditions, taking singing lessons, and hoping that somehow my break would come.

Linda Hansen

One of my co-workers, an usher at the theater, was another starving performer . . . **Al Pacino.** Al had a very good friend in those days, and the two of them would often come to the movie theater before Al had to be there and do silly stuff on the street. One night, Al did a pratfall in front of the theater, and people who saw it were concerned about his welfare. I sat there laughing, as I knew that Al and his friend were just messing around. Al and I met when I was twenty, and as we worked the same evening shift, when we got off work, he would usually walk me home. We would sit in my apartment, smoking pot, all hours of the night, just hanging out. No, we never had a romantic interest in each other. We were just friends. When we first started working together, I was living in an apartment on 1st Avenue, between 61st and 62nd, and eventually I moved to my apartment on West 72nd Street, where I lived until I left New York at age twenty-six.

Al and I stayed friends during those six years. We were both fired from the movie theater, and then I got a job working in the men's clothing industry (more about this later), and Al would get jobs as a super at different apartment buildings. The benefit of being a super, free rent was part of the salary. Al would come by my 72nd Street apartment, and we continued to hang out. There was a time when he was auditioning for the Actors Studio, and he would come over so I could run lines with him as he worked on his audition piece. He often had parties at his various apartments, and I was always invited to attend. During these years, Al started to get work off-Broadway, started winning awards, and getting recognition. In November of 1970, Al was filming his first movie role in *The Panic in Needle Park*. At that time, Needle Park was the nickname for a park that was at the corner of Broadway and 72nd Street, down the block from my apartment. I used to take the bus to and from my job on Avenue of the Americas, still working in the men's clothing industry, and would get off the bus at that corner. On my last night in New York, I got off the bus and walked to the diner that was at the corner of 71st Street and Broadway, where a scene for the movie was being filmed. I had spoken with Al to tell him I was leaving New York, and he told me to stop by the set. I waited outside, and finally, there was a break in the filming. Al was sitting in a booth in the diner, which was part of the scene, and he knew I was going to be stopping by to say goodbye. He looked up, saw me standing outside, and motioned for me to come in and sit down with him. We sat and talked until they were ready to start shooting again. He had a rose for me; we gave each other hugs and said goodbye. Little did I know my friend of so many years was going to become such an important star.

72ND STREET

PETER MAX

I was a young woman living in New York City in the winter of 1965. I had been living in a one-room/studio apartment on the East Side when I was told the landlord was not renewing my lease. After scouring the "apartment for lease" ads in the New York Times, I eventually found a two-room apartment on the West Side. I had been living at 1123 1st Avenue, and this was a big move for me—from the East Side to the West Side. The ad had been written in a very unique manner and talked about being "a cool pad with a mural on the wall." The ad caught my attention, so I went to see it. It had been the apartment of an artist.

As the apartment was a sublet and not a direct rental, the current tenant, **Peter Max**, had to take me to the landlord of the building. When it came time to sign the lease, the landlord looked at me and asked if I was over twenty-one. I started to panic as I was only twenty, but before I could say anything, Peter looked at him and responded, "Of course, she is. I wouldn't have brought her here if she wasn't." I signed the lease.

I don't think the artist who did the mural was famous. I never knew who the artist was, but it was not done by Peter. I always thought it might have been done by his graphic design partner, Tom Daly. At the time, they had created a graphic of Toulouse-Lautrec that had the name "Daly & Max" in Lautrec's bow tie. They had received some notoriety for this image. I decided to rent the apartment after seeing it, and when I took possession of the apartment, a poster of this graphic had been left taped on a wall.

During the next one-and-a-half years, about once every month or two, the buzzer to my twelfth-floor apartment would ring; it would be anywhere from midnight to 2 a.m., and it would be Peter. I was twenty years old when this started, and thought nothing of getting out of bed, putting on clothes, and going downstairs. We would go riding in Peter's blue Karmann Ghia, and we would ride around New York City for an hour or two. Sometimes we would get pizza, Chinese food, or freshly made bagels, and we would talk about anything and everything. I cannot tell you why he chose to make me a friend, but we were friends. Eventually, the doorbell stopped ringing. Our friendship waned for no specific reason. I don't know why, other than he was starting to get a lot of exciting work, and he was starting on the road to his success. During this time, Peter dropped a lot of acid, which I think is understandable when looking at his art. He would ask me to do this with him, but I always said no. There were so many stories about bad acid trips, and I was afraid of having a bad experience. This also may have been a reason for the end of our friendship.

Over the next few years, Peter and his partner dissolved their graphic design studio, and Peter was working on his own. He started to gain some fame and designed the interior of a restaurant in Manhattan. He was beginning to become the famous Peter Max. I called and asked if he was the one and the same, and congratulated him on the success he was achieving. We laughed and met for a coffee, and then continued our separate ways.

During the six years that I lived in the apartment at 121 W. 72nd Street, the forgotten poster stayed taped to the door of my bedroom closet. Over time, it had torn in several places, and I thought nothing of it. I left the apartment in November of 1970 and moved back to St. Louis. The poster was left, still taped to the closet door in my bedroom.

Rubbing Shoulders

Sometime around 1974–75, there was a small art gallery in St. Louis, and they hosted a one-man show for the now-famous Peter Max. I went to the opening, and it was packed, wall to wall, with customers and friends. What followed next left me stunned . . . The small gallery was very crowded, and as I walked in, surrounded by people from the back of the gallery, Peter Max yelled out, "Linda!" He pushed his way past everyone to greet me with a huge hug as if I were his best friend. I was shocked and flattered.

We talked for quite a while, during which time he talked about the day when he took me to the landlord of the apartment building to make the arrangements for the sublet. What shocked me the most was when he brought up what I wore that day, ten years earlier. I said, "I can't believe you remember what I was wearing!"

Peter's response was a lesson I have never forgotten. "Were you there that day?" I replied, "Of course." He said, "Well, I was, too. If you remember that day, why do you think I would not? Just because I am now famous, it doesn't take away my memories." This was a lesson I have never forgotten. My mother always told me, "It doesn't matter who someone is, we all put our pants on the same way, one leg at a time!" I had forgotten her often-said adage, and here was Peter telling me about the same thing in different words.

Peter and I did not see each other again until almost thirty years later. Once again, he had come to St. Louis for a one-man show. By this time, Peter was truly a famous artist. He was having a one-man show at a gallery inside a shopping mall. My husband and I knew where he would enter the building for his appearance, and we waited for a short while before we saw him. The years had taken their toll on Peter, and sadly, he looked ravaged from his lifestyle. I walked up to him and introduced myself. At this meeting, he did not immediately remember me, but I then mentioned the address of the apartment. At the mention of this address, he immediately looked at me, and a glimmer of recognition showed on his face.

We spent the next hour with Peter at the reception, having our picture taken with him and laughing about where our lives had taken us. We talked as if almost no time had passed. He asked if I still had the poster! I said no, that it had been torn and taped to the closet door and had been left behind when I had moved. He looked at me, smiled slyly, and said, "Too bad. It would be worth a lot of money today." No, there is no Peter Max in my home, but the times I shared with him live on in my memories.

MORE 72ND STREET

Some time frames overlap one another, as do some of the friendships. Of course, we all have more than one friend, and everyone I have talked about were all friends or acquaintances.

Sorry, this is not a "who I slept with" story. Sometime during the mid-1960s, when I was living on 72nd Street, I had a wonderful little black Pomeranian named Char. Actually, I had two Pomeranians. First, there was Hans. He had a heart condition and died at four years old; then Char came into my life. Char was a fun little character. I taught him how to walk off-lead (leash), and he was great at listening to me. Char knew he had to obey the New York City "curb your dog" rule, and he would jump into the gutter to do his business. As we would approach a street corner, I would say, "Street, wait," and Char would just stand there and wait for me to get to the corner. At this point, when we had the green light, I would say, "Hurry, crossing," and Char would run across the street, get to the corner, and then turn around to look at me and wait for me to get where he was. In retrospect, this was amazing considering all the traffic in New York City, but that is what we did.

We would walk from my apartment to Central Park almost every weekend; sometimes we would hang out at the famous fountain, and other times we would go to one of the fields, and I would sunbathe with the many other New Yorkers who were doing the same thing. New York

City in the mid-1960s was an incredible place. People were friendly, and everyone would talk to each other. On one of these Saturdays, a man and his children came over to chat because his young daughter was fascinated by Char. After several Saturdays of chatting in the park, he eventually asked me for coffee, lunch, etc. I kept waiting for him to make a move on me, but he never did. We were just friends. He eventually invited me to a cocktail party that he told me was going to be very fancy, and I was excited to go. The day before the party, he called and told me he was sick and was going to be unable to take me. I was sad to miss what appeared to be an exciting opportunity, but I was relieved, as I did not have the appropriate clothes to attend a fancy cocktail party. So, part of me gave a great sigh of relief. But . . . he said he really wanted me to go and that he had a particularly good friend who was going, and this man did not have a date. My friend wanted to know if it was okay for him to give my number to the other man, and that he would take me. Once again, my naivety was there, and I said yes. Thus, Kurt Chambre entered my life.

Kurt was a dashing man. He was German-born, had been in the United States for many years, and was a successful clothing manufacturer. Kurt owned a company that made expensive men's slacks, which were sold in the better stores throughout the United States. He looked like Aristotle Onassis with white hair, and he had a deep golden tan twelve months a year. Kurt called me at work and told me what time he would pick me up. I wore a borrowed black dress, and my purse was borrowed from the same friend. The only things I wore that I owned were my underwear, shoes, and a strand of pearls . . . I still own the strand of pearls. The pearls had been my mother's, and she had given them to me. I did not find out until the mid-1980s that the pearls were real and were quite valuable! Kurt picked me up, and I had my first ride in a limousine! I was trying so hard to be sophisticated and not look like the overwhelmed and excited twenty-three-year-old that I was.

Linda Hansen

The party in and of itself was just a cocktail party. I have no memories of it, but this was my first date with Kurt, which then led to an almost two-year friendship. In many ways, it was much more than friendship, but it was not sexual. I used to see Kurt an average of four or five nights a week! In the two years of our friendship, I can only think of one time when he came to my apartment, which was when I was sick with the flu and had a high fever. He came by in the afternoon with chicken soup, flowers, and lots of books. For our dates, I usually went to his apartment, which was very large and beautiful, on Park Avenue in the 30s. I would meet him there, and then we would go to dinner, the movies, parties, or whatever else was planned. There were times he would have me meet him at the restaurant where we were going to have dinner, or he would have me meet him at a movie theater, if this was better timing for us both. When our evening was over, most of the time, he would hail a cab and give me $20–$50 to pay for the cab. He would only take me home if we had been uptown. Of course, I was expected to keep the change!

What he was doing was making sure that I had money to go shopping and buy the clothes I needed, so we could go to all the places he was taking me. It was sort of like being a kept woman without the sex and without his totally supporting me. Kurt was just making sure that I would not be embarrassed. He used to tell me the reason he liked dating me was that he was twenty-seven years older than me, and he liked having a cute young girl on his arm. He also liked that I was smart and had the ability to chat with anybody, at anytime, anywhere, and on any subject. As he once said, "I can take you to dinner with the bank president, and when it is time to say 'fuck,' you say 'fuck'. I know you will always hold your own, and you will never embarrass me."

I loved my friendship with Kurt. He would sometimes go on a cruise and be gone two months, and he would travel for business, but we usually saw each other four to five nights a week . . . except on Friday nights. Friday night was one of the nights I did not see Kurt. He played in a weekly poker game with a group of friends. The men would go from one player's apartment/home to the next. When it was Kurt's time, he would have me there to be his hostess and serve beverages and snacks. Most of the other men were married or had live-in girlfriends. If he lost, he lost, but when he won, he would give me 20 percent of his winnings every week. It was a wild and crazy friendship.

Christmas came, and he gave me a beautiful Pucci dress. I was so excited as I knew how expensive it was. I could not believe it. He had me put it right on and then took me to one of the most incredible house parties I had ever been to. This party was hosted by a famous New York City radio personality, **Fred Robbins**. His Christmas Party was the party to which people wished to be invited. I can no longer name all the famous actors, musicians, athletes, politicians, and other well-known people who were there, but it was a who's who of the mid-1960s. One of the important people there, and why I am telling this story, was **Rod Steiger**. Another brief encounter, the memory of which has lasted a lifetime.

I used to smoke at the time, and Kurt had given me a gold Dunhill lighter, which was *the* lighter to own. I was sitting on a sofa in the living room, Kurt was off somewhere talking to people he knew, and I sat quietly watching all the famous people at the party in total awe and disbelief that this was where I was . . . it was a "pinch me" moment. My pack of Marlboros and my Dunhill were on the end table next to me, and sitting at a right angle to the same sofa, next to the end table, was Rod Steiger! Like a scene from a bad movie, he leaned over and asked, "Are these yours?" I said, "Yes." He said, "May I?" The bad movie scene continued as I picked up the pack of cigarettes, extended one from the pack so he could take it, and then I lit his cigarette. Hokey!

The next thing I knew was that he sat there and chatted with me about all sorts of things for about half an hour until dinner was served. He had dinner in one room while Kurt and I had dinner in another. After dinner, Kurt told me we were going to leave. I must say I was disappointed, as I wanted to stay longer, but I knew when Kurt said we were leaving, we were leaving. We walked into the dining room, where the host was sitting at a very long table, so that Kurt could say good night. At the far end of the table was Rod Steiger, and as we started to walk away, in his most unique voice, he said, "Good night, young lady." The memory of that evening is as if it were yesterday.

The following Tuesday, Kurt called me at work to tell me that I had been the hit of the party. Really! Kurt said that Fred Robbins had called him, saying that several of the men who had been at the party had wanted to know who I was and that they had asked if there was a way they could contact me. So . . . Fred called Kurt, and Kurt called me. Now, keep in mind that I said my relationship with Kurt was not sexual, so he did not care if I wanted to meet any of these men. He liked the fact that I was such a hit, especially as I was wearing my new Pucci dress that he had just given me. So, Kurt gave Fred my number.

CY COLEMAN

One of the men who had asked for my phone number was **Cy Coleman**, a well-known music writer and composer of many hit singles, and music for Broadway and movies. I was so excited. Cy did call, and Cy and I dated for about six to nine months. Like Kurt, I saw Cy several nights a week. He would take me to dinner, to movies, to cocktail parties, and to black-tie affairs. Once again, my ability to talk to anybody about anything is what Cy liked about me. Cy introduced me to so many famous people. He would often take me to the Algonquin Hotel, where there was a small cabaret, and we would go to hear **Mabel Mercer**. She was a good friend of his and sang quite a few of his songs. Between sets, she would come and sit at our table. I used to pinch myself and think I could not believe what was happening. I was a huge fan of hers and owned several of her albums . . . I still have them. On another evening, we went to a black-tie party at the Waldorf Astoria Hotel in honor of **Ed Sullivan**. It seemed that everywhere Cy took me, I was going to meet famous celebrities. Too bad I did not keep a diary!

THE FOUR SEASONS

Other small moments comprised my life during these years. I was still hoping to become a singer during the mid-1960s. I had a personal manager who I thought was going to make the difference, but this never happened. Perhaps one of the reasons she had no time for me was that she was the manager for **The Four Seasons**! At the time, I was working for a clothing manufacturer, Arthur H. Freedberg. The Four Seasons were already big stars, but everyone always wants to get something for a deal. They wanted new blazers to wear on stage. Freedberg was known for making high-end men's clothing, and I arranged for them to come to our office and pick out the blazer they wanted. I remember being surprised by their choice as they chose what I thought was an ugly shade of green, and I could not understand why.

The jackets arrived at the office, and The Four Seasons came back a second time to pick them up. A brief time later, they did a performance in Central Park, and I was invited to see them perform in their new jackets. Our manager invited me to come backstage before the show. This was still in the days when performers were much more accessible than they are now. I was taken backstage before the performance, hung out in the dressing room, and spent the evening with them.

Part IV

The author, Lady with Many Faces

BACK TO ST. LOUIS: MAKEUP LADY WITH MANY FACES

I moved back to St. Louis in November 1970 and was married the following month. My starter husband was a hair stylist who had been trained by **Paul Mitchell**, who had been the style director and part of the Vidal Sassoon design team, and later went on to develop a brand of hair care products. We opened a salon in St. Louis and were trendsetters in the early 1970s in St. Louis. During these years, Paul came to St. Louis several times for hair shows, and we always saw him. We would pick him up at the airport, take him to his hotel, and have dinner with him. There came a time when Paul was going to London, England, to introduce a new permanent wave product. He invited a group of us to go on this trip, at our expense. My starter husband and I went, as we had never been to England and wanted to take advantage of the opportunity. One day, while Paul was demonstrating the permanent wave product, he asked me to take the model upstairs, finish the job, and bring her back down when done. I was not a hairdresser. Paul knew this, but he asked me anyway. I went to the stage, got the model, and started to walk away with her. Fortunately, one of the other haircutters on this trip came up to me and said that he would take her. He knew I wasn't a hairstylist!

I had a skill for business, having grown up with a family-owned business, and oversaw the advertising and development of the business. Because of my theatrical training, it was an easy transition for me to bring makeup into the salon. I was divorced in 1978, and lost my business, as the name of the salon was my husband's name, leaving me adrift with no source of income. I called St. Louis Magazine and presented the idea of doing a local fashion column. Don't ask me why I did this, as I had never written before, but I needed to work so I could support myself. To my excitement, they said yes, and for a year, I wrote a monthly two-page story. It was because of this that my next career evolved.

There was a Neiman-Marcus store in St. Louis at this time, and the owner, **Stanley Marcus**, had come to town. I had an appointment to interview him for my magazine column. While I was with him, he said how he liked to have things that are made in that city. I asked him if he had ever had Switzer's licorice. He replied that he had not, and I explained that it was a locally made product. The next day, I went and bought some and put it in a package and took it to the store for him.

My career as a makeup artist for film and video started in July of 1980. I was called by a friend who asked if I knew how to do makeup for TV. Of course, I replied yes. I knew how to do it for the stage; I had taught makeup in the salon and had done it for the photo shoots for the magazine. I thought, how different could it be? I worked as a makeup artist for film and video from 1980 until 2002–3. The list of people for whom I did makeup during these years is long. I can't remember the names of everyone with whom I worked, but for the time you work with someone as their makeup artist, the relationship is close and friendly. You are taking care of them and are in their physical space in a way that is usually for family, loved ones, and doctors. Sometimes I worked with someone for just a few hours, sometimes it was for several days, and sometimes the relationship would last for a period of years.

In 1981, while working on another TV commercial for the local NBC station in St. Louis, I met **George Noory,** who was the news director at that time. He hired me to teach makeup to all the on-air talent. George went on to be the host of the radio show, *Coast to Coast AM*. Unlike the big TV markets of New York and Los Angeles, St. Louis did not have a makeup artist at the station. My work with the station continued for many years as they continued to hire me whenever they hired a new on-air personality and anytime they had someone of importance at the station.

Because of my relationship with KSDK, there was a time when NBC was coming to St. Louis, and they asked George for the name of their makeup artist. Of course, he gave them my name and contact information. This then led to a variety of jobs, but two are of interest.

On July 2, 1984, the *Today Show* came to St. Louis to do a live show at the base of the St. Louis Arch. I was expected to work with the on-air personalities of the show and all the guests. **Jane Pauley** was nice but didn't want me to make her up, as she told me she did her own. **Willard Scott** was friendly and fun to work with. **Bryant Gumbel** needed attention often. He has a spot in the center of his lower lip that does not have the same pigment color as the rest of his lip. He expressed concern as to my ability to make it all look the same as his makeup artist in New York was able to do, and I said it would not be a problem. He was happy with the outcome, but I had to touch him up at almost every commercial break. We all tend to lick our lips when speaking, and the makeup would lighten, which required me to have to touch it up. In the end, all went well.

I can't remember all the guests of that show, but I clearly remember two of them. I made up **John Denver**, the well-known country and folk singer, who was one of the handsomest men I had ever made up. He was incredibly pleasant and easy to chat with. I made up quite a lot of people that day, and one other person stands out in my mind. I had to make up **Chuck Berry**, who was a pioneer of rock 'n' roll. I couldn't believe how physically dirty he was. I did everything I could to stand as far away as possible from him and immediately threw everything out that I had used while working on him. Some of the people with whom I spent time were wonderful, while some of them were less than pleasant. He was not unpleasant to me, but he was certainly the dirtiest person I had ever made up.

Linda Hansen

On October 11, 1992, one of the Bush vs Clinton debates was held at Washington University in St. Louis. Again, I received a phone call from NBC, and they hired me to make up **George Stephanopoulos,** who was going to be on *Meet the Press* that Sunday morning. At that time, Mr. Stephanopoulos was the communications director for the Clinton campaign. While I was making him up in the room that had been provided, someone from the Secret Service came in and told us we had to leave the room. I explained what I was doing, and the agent responded that he didn't care and that we had to leave the room. I quickly packed my small on-set bag, and George Stephanopoulos and I left the room and found a hallway in which I could finish my job. When I was finally given permission to return to my room, it became clear that it had been thoroughly searched, as everything in my makeup box had been removed and was all over the room. It was a most interesting experience. At one point, while I was waiting to go back into my room, one of the Secret Service agents and his dog came up the stairs to where I was sitting. I was amazed at how intense this working dog was, and the handler told me the dog was working at that moment, and I should not make any attempt to pet it.

I did makeup for athletes, politicians, singers, actors, TV personalities, many corporate CEOs, and everyday people. Some of those I made up during my career include:

POLITICIANS	**ATHLETES**
John Ashcroft	Lou Brock
Christopher 'Kit' Bond	Wilt Chamberlain
Tom Eggleton	Dan Dierdorf
Richard 'Dick' Gephardt	Whitey Herzog
Vince Schoemehl	Jackie Joyner Kersey
Harriet Woods	Stan Musial

Darrell Porter
Mike Shannon
Ozzie Smith

SINGERS
Chuck Berry
Rosemary Clooney
John Denver
Four Tops
B. B. King

ACTORS
Richard Crenna
Cyd Charisse
Sammy Davis, Jr.
Chad Everett
John Forsyth
Alice Ghostly
Peter Graves
Andy Griffith
Carol Kane
Ben Murphy
Avery Schreiber
Betty Thomas
Joey Travolta
Margaret Travolta

TV PERSONALTIES
Dr. Joyce Brothers
Jack Buck
Dick Cavett
Bob Costas
Dick Enberg
Bryant Gumbel
Skitch Henderson
Wink Martindale
Ed McMahon
Jane Pauley
Sally Jesse Raphael
Pat Sajak
Willard Scott
George Stephanopoulos
Alex Trebek
Ben Vereen
Vanna White

Cyd Charisse

Lou Brock

The author and Richard Crenna

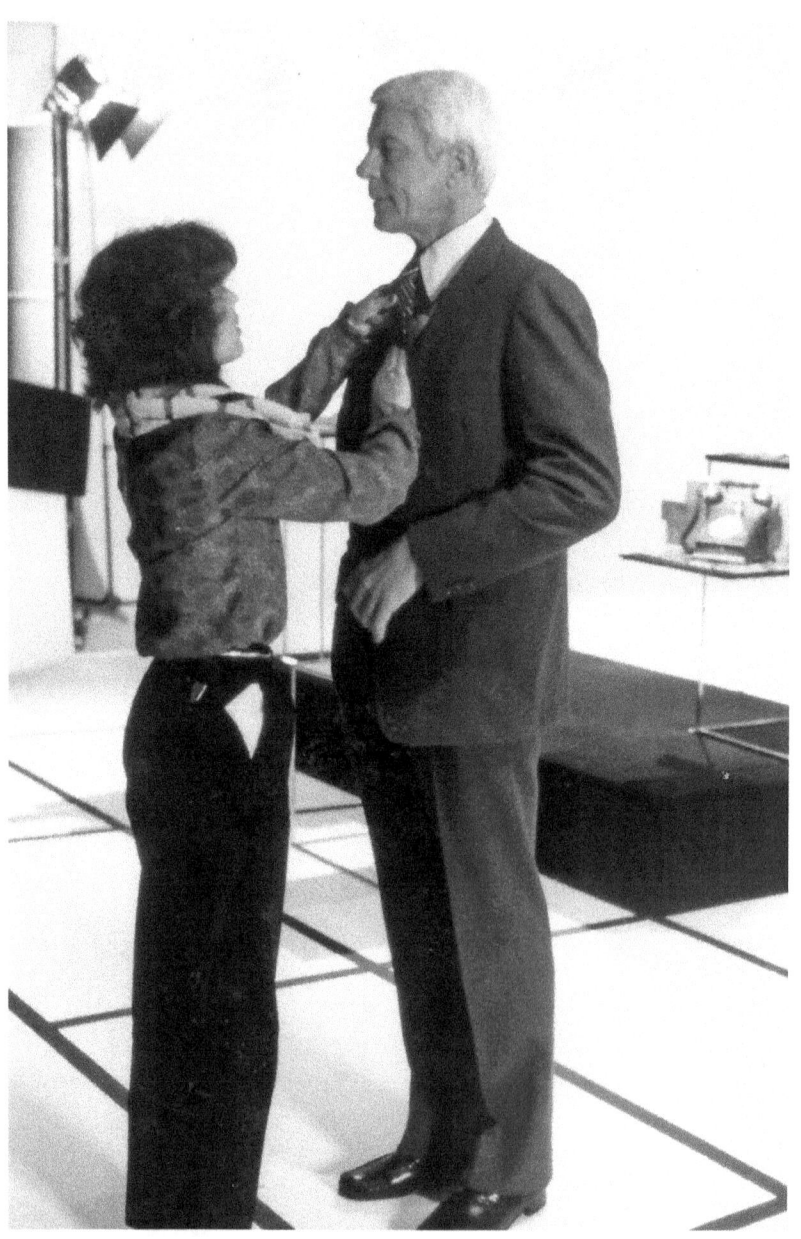

Above and right, the author with Peter Graves

PETER GRAVES AND OTHERS

I had been working as a makeup artist for about two years when I was hired by Maritz, a large company based in St. Louis, for the first time. Maritz did incentive work for many major firms, and part of the work Maritz did was to make corporate videos. They had not regularly hired makeup artists, but they needed one for this particular job. I was hired to make up **Peter Graves**. I was so excited. This was the first time I was going to make up a star. Not only had he been famous, but when I was young, he starred in the TV show *Fury*, and I had been a big fan. I worked with Peter numerous times over the next several years. Each job usually lasted about three days.

It is far too easy to make idle gossip about personalities. I think it is sad that part of fame brings the curiosity of the public, and often at the most thoughtless of times. I had been invited by Peter Graves to go to dinner with the producer of the project and some of the other people involved. While we were eating, a woman came to the table and asked Peter

for his autograph. He graciously put down his fork and knife and signed his name on the piece of paper she had. When she left, I turned to Peter and commented on how rude I thought it was of her to approach him while he was eating. His response was that he was a public figure and that without people knowing who he was and wanting to see him, he would have no career. He said he considered this to be the price of fame. I had the pleasure of working with Peter for over two years, and whenever the client and producers took him to dinner, he would be sure I was included.

My work at Maritz gave me the opportunity to work with a variety of people who were well known at that time; one person was **Andy Griffith**. I was known for being friendly and able to chat with anyone about anything. He came with his manager, and it became very clear to me that he had no interest in talking with me and so I made sure to do my job but not try to develop a relationship with him. He had recently been very ill with Guillain-Barré syndrome and still was not feeling well. We worked together for two days. On the third day of the shoot, the crew shot on location in downtown St. Louis and not at the studio of Maritz. During the afternoon, Mr. Griffith came to the shoot to say goodbye to the crew. He made a point of approaching me and thanking me for working with him. I thought this was the nicest gesture, and I told him that I hoped he would continue to feel better.

I got to know **Lou Rawls** and, on another evening, when several of us were out, someone approached Lou with a wet napkin and asked for his autograph. Lou gave this woman a big smile and told her if she would come back with a piece of paper, he would gladly give her his autograph. She did not return. Lou looked at me and said that he was happy to give autographs, but that if he signs on a wet napkin, we all know where that autograph will end up . . . in the trash!

Most of the work I did was for film and/or video, but there were times I worked on print shoots. I had been hired to work with **B.B. King** for a day. He was gentle, friendly, and considerate. As the day came to an end, he asked if I would like to attend his concert that night, and he arranged for me to have two tickets to attend the performance he was doing. He also gave me a lapel pin of his famous guitar, Lucille, which I hate to say, like many other things, didn't come to Florida when I retired.

ED MCMAHON

I had several print photographers who hired me on a regular basis. One day, I was hired to work with **Ed McMahon** who was known for being Johnny Carson's sidekick on the Tonight Show. He could not have been nicer, and we spent the morning chatting. He had left to go back to his hotel when I saw he had left his sports jacket at the studio. I knew where he was staying as we had talked about it, and I told the company that had hired me that I would take the jacket to him. I got to the hotel, asked for him at the reception desk, and they told me he was in the restaurant having lunch. I was taken to his table, told him about the jacket, and he invited me to have lunch with him and his wife. Once again, I had the opportunity to spend my time with another nice and down-to-earth person.

The author and Ed McMahon

The author with Ed McMahon and stage crew

The author with Chad Everett

CHAD EVERETT

Working with **Chad Everett** for a day, who appeared in many movies and TV shows, turned out to bring unexpected fun. The shoot wrapped early. He was spending the night in St. Louis, and I offered to take him to his hotel. The director was thrilled that I was going to take him from the location, rather than have him spend time sitting around and doing nothing. There was a lot of time left in the day, so I asked him if he would like to see some of St. Louis. Chad said he had never been to St. Louis before, and he was happy to do so. I spent the afternoon being his tour guide, drove him through some of the distinctive neighborhoods, and we ended the day by going to the St. Louis Arch. As we left the arch, he asked if I would like to have dinner with him. Thoughtfully, he had me invite my boyfriend, who is now my husband, to meet us, but he was unable to do so due to a work commitment.

Several months passed, and it was Memorial Day weekend. My boyfriend and I were spending a quiet weekend doing work around the condominium in which we lived when the phone rang. A man didn't introduce himself but asked if this was his favorite makeup artist. I was taken aback and asked who this was. He replied, "Chad." He had already come to town for the shoot we were doing in the morning, and he was sitting in his hotel room. I asked what he was doing for dinner, and he replied, "Nothing." So, I asked if he would like to join us for dinner, but that it would be nothing more than barbecued chicken. He said he would be happy to do so. I gave him our address, and we set the time that we would expect him. I hung up and went running to Gary. "You won't believe what just happened. We are having a dinner guest." I did not have enough food for our guest, so I ran to the grocery store and bought more. The time came, the doorbell rang, and there was Chad with a beautiful houseplant. We ate dinner on our deck and then sat there chatting. Finally, I looked at him and said that I probably needed to take him back to the hotel, as we had a very early call in the morning, and his body schedule was going to be way off as he was still on California time. This was a multi-day shoot and included our going to Indianapolis to shoot at a hospital. He had been famous as Dr. Joe Gannon in the TV series *Medical Center*. The staff at the hospital in Indianapolis went crazy as he walked the halls during the on-location shoot.

SAMMY DAVIS—PART THREE

Finally, a time came when I worked with Sammy Davis as his makeup artist. The Variety Club in St. Louis held an annual telethon fundraising event. There was often a major performer as the star of the show, and then many other well-known performers were there to assist. Sammy Davis hosted the show in 1984, and I was hired to take care of him. He was as outgoing, friendly, and wonderful as I had always imagined he would be. I told him of my two other brief encounters with him, causing much laughter. I worked with him for six or more hours. I always had to keep an eye on him, and in between performances, at quiet moments, I would approach him to dry perspiration and powder him so he would not be shiny on camera. There were times that he would look at me, do a silly dance, or say something to me. He was one of the nicest and most charming people with whom I worked.

I did the job with the Variety Club for several years and did not keep track of the people with whom I worked, but one year, **John Forsythe** was there. While making him up, I told him the story about his son, Dall. He was surprised when I told him that I had worked with Dall that one summer. Dall had developed a relationship with one of the dancers at the theater. They were married sometime later, and Mr. Forsythe told me they were still married . . . over forty years at the time. Mr. Forsythe was polite and professional, and he certainly knew how to make me feel good. He was shocked that I knew Dall from 1962 and said he could not believe I was old enough to have had the experience I shared. The world is indeed small.

BOB COSTAS

People often ask me, "Who is the nicest person you have met?" This is an easy question to answer as there is one person who, hands down, is one of the finest people I am privileged to know and to call a friend. I first met Bob in the spring of 1982. Bob had worked a golf tournament with **Jay Randolph**, a St. Louis sports reporter who did national golf reporting. While Bob and Jay were working together, Bob saw Jay putting on makeup. Bob asked how he knew what he was doing, and Jay explained there was this gal in St. Louis who worked with the on-air reporters at the NBC station where he worked and had taught them all how to apply their own makeup, and the station provided the makeup. Bob had come to St. Louis, where he used to live, to call a baseball game, and Jay gave him my phone number. Bob called me, explained what he needed, and I told him that it would be easy to do. He came to my condominium; I gave him a lesson and sold him the makeup and other supplies he would need to take care of himself when he was on the road.

On Sunday, October 10, 1982, my phone rang, and I heard, "Hi, this is Bob, Bob Costas." Now, Bob has a unique voice, and it is not one that someone would not recognize, but this is an example of how humble he is. He wanted to know if I was available to work with him early the next morning. The St. Louis Cardinals had made it to the World Series, and he was coming to town to work for NBC and the telecast. I met Bob at six in the morning at the stadium for him to tape a portion for the evening show. As we were saying goodbye, he said, "Can you come back this afternoon to work with me for the evening show?" I said, "Yes." Before I knew what was happening, I was given all the credentials from NBC that would get me into the stadium that night. Working with Bob during the World Series led to a working relationship that went on for over twenty years, until the early 2000s. I never traveled with Bob, but when Bob was in St. Louis and working, I would be working, too.

Bob was the Emcee for a large fundraising event for a children's hospital in St. Louis. For two years, he had me come to make him up for the show. One year, my husband and I were in the room he used backstage, waiting for him. While we were there, a man came into the room and said, "Hi, I'm Jay, **Jay Leno**." My husband looked at him and said, "No kidding!" Jay laughed, chatted with us for a few moments, and then he asked where Bob was. I explained that I was his makeup artist, and I would let Bob know he was looking for him.

The following year, **Tony Bennett** was the co-headliner. Bob provided us with tickets so that we could see his performance. I went backstage after the show to thank Bob and found myself standing next to Mr. Bennett. This was one of the rare times that I acted like a gushing fan. I was so excited. I spoke with him briefly to tell him what a big fan I was and how great it was to see him perform. Then I told him that I had taken my mother to see him at a performance in Brooklyn sometime in the mid-1960s. He looked at me and told me when and where it was!

The public has no idea of Bob's extreme kindness and generosity. In 1995, I started working with a small nonprofit, for which I eventually served as the executive director for nineteen years. For several years, I could work full time and still work with Bob. Eventually, the working relationship with Bob ended because my work schedule often interfered with times when he needed me, but not the friendship. Bob made annual donations to the charity, and at times the donations were not casual donations, but large amounts. He honored me with a donation in honor of my retirement when the time came for me to close that chapter of my life.

Bob misses nothing. The St. Louis Post-Dispatch did a story about my husband, Gary, and how he overcame challenges in his life. Gary was sitting at our kitchen table, drinking coffee, and reading the morning newspaper when the phone rang. Gary said, "Hello," and the voice on the other end said, "Gary, hi, this is Bob . . . Bob Costas." Of course, Gary recognized the voice and wondered why Bob was calling him. Bob had called Gary to compliment him on the article. Gary was shocked. With all the people Bob knew and could call, he had taken the time to call Gary. Bob truly is one of the most amazing and thoughtful people I know.

Bob's kindness and humanity were always present. Our relationship became a twenty-year professional friendship. One day, Bob arrived for a shoot a little late, which was most unusual. As we worked together, I sensed something was on his mind, and so I gave him space and did not try to chat with him as usual. When the shoot was over, as always, he politely said goodbye. The next day I got home from my job with the nonprofit, and there was a message on my home answering machine. I listened to it, and there was Bob, apologizing for not having treated me well the day before! I called him and said he treated me with his usual courtesy and that he had no need to apologize.

My life, and that of my husband's, became more and more involved with our nonprofit. Our organization had been selected by another group to be the recipient of their major fundraiser. They asked if I knew of anyone who might be willing to be the guest host of the event. I asked Bob if he was going to be in St. Louis, and would it be possible for him to do this? Bob graciously said, "Yes." Several weeks prior to the event, Bob called and said his schedule had changed and he was not going to be in St. Louis as he had thought. Typical of the quality of man he is, he offered to do a video that could be played at the start of the evening. He had become a true friend over the years we worked together.

If you asked me to say something about Bob that is not nice, I am unable to do so. He is truly one of the nicest people I have ever known, but if pushed, I can say one thing about him. He has one of the most amazing vocabularies of anyone I have ever known. The way he speaks when on camera is the way he speaks during any conversation he is having. I used to laugh that every time I got home from working with Bob, I had to get out my dictionary and look up the words he used that I didn't know.

Linda Hansen

ST. LOUIS CARDINALS

OZZIE SMITH

Living in St. Louis, I often worked on TV commercials and industrial films with many of the St. Louis Cardinals (baseball), as opposed to the St. Louis Cardinals (football). I cannot begin to think of how many times I was at the stadium to work. I worked on the field, in the restaurant, and in the locker room, and I even knew Doggie, the guard of the locker room.

One of the nicest players I had the opportunity to work with was **Ozzie Smith**. He was at the height of his success in the 1980s. He was often cast in TV commercials, and I also worked on a video of his life. I met his wife, his children, and his mother. Ozzie was always a polite, gentle, and pleasant person. Almost twenty years later, Ozzie opened a restaurant in St. Louis County. It was extremely popular, near where I worked, and I ate there often. On one of my visits, Ozzie happened to be there. I walked up to where he was sitting and reintroduced myself. He immediately responded as if we had just worked together. I told him about the non-profit I oversaw and explained that we were getting a fundraising event prepared and that I needed silent auction items. Ozzie was quick to offer some memorabilia. He kindly made donations for many years thereafter.

DARRYL PORTER

There was a chain of pizza restaurants in St. Louis in the 1980s called Pantera's. For a while they used **Darryl Porter**, catcher for the Cardinals, as their spokesperson. I worked with him several times. On one of these times, Darryl was putting some chewing tobacco into his mouth. I was standing next to him when he looked at me and said, "Would you like a dip?" Darryl was from Oklahoma and had a real Southern drawl, making his question even more charming and funny. I looked at him and replied, "No, thank you. The only time I dip is when I'm dancing." We both shared a good laugh. Sadly, Darryl died when he was fifty years old.

GEORGE HENDRICK

When I was working with Bob Costas at the 1982 World Series, prior to the start of the game, Bob and I were walking in the tunnel to where the locker room and other offices were, so I could make him up for the game. As I was entering the tunnel, a tall, thin player and another man came walking towards me. As they were coming from the dark, I was unable to know who they were, but as I got closer, the player was saying something about "those fuckers." I kept walking, met Bob, put his makeup on, and then came back out to sit on the player's bench. I would sit on the player's bench before the start of each game to be near Bob so that I could make sure he looked good for his time on camera. As the start of the game approached, a few of the players started to come out and sit on the bench. After a while, this tall young man, who was sitting a few feet away from me, looked at me and said, "Excuse me, ma'am, are you the woman I saw in the tunnel?" I said that I was, and then he apologized to me for the language he had used. I smiled and said he did not have to worry and that I had heard that word many times before. We then sat and chatted until the game started. The next night, I was sitting in the same spot when my new friend came and sat right next to me. "Hi, I'm George." I said, "Hi, I'm Linda." We spent the time chatting until the game started. The games then went out of town, but they returned to St. Louis for the seventh and final game of the series. Again, I was sitting on the players' bench when George came over and sat down next to me. As we chatted, he asked if I would like an autographed ball. When I said yes, he said, "I'll be right back." When he returned, he put a hand-autographed team ball into my hands. Many autographed baseballs have stamped signatures, but this one was all signed by hand. I did not realize that my new friend was **George Hendrick,** who played in Major League Baseball as an outfielder, between 1971 and 1988. He was called Silent George, because he was supposed to not be talkative and didn't like to do interviews. Well, you could not prove that to me. To me, George was always pleasant, warm, friendly, and inquisitive.

Linda Hansen

WHITEY HERZOG

I cannot remember how many times I was around Coach **Whitey Herzog**. I would be at the stadium for news interviews, commercials, and short films. I was there so often that Doggie, the security man at the locker room entrance, knew who I was. On this occasion, I was there to film a commercial with Whitey, which meant I had to make him up and take care of him for the time I was there. At one point, while I was in his office preparing for the next shot, he asked me if I would go to Chicago with him! He explained that it would be an afternoon game, which meant that we would be able to have a wonderful dinner afterwards. I smiled and politely said, "No, thank you." Whitey was married, and I would never have compromised my job by behaving in such an inappropriate manner. I am far from a prude, but I had a policy of not dating married men or dating men with whom I worked.

MIKE SHANNON

Mike Shannon was the most despicable person with whom I ever worked. He played third base and right field for the St. Louis Cardinals from 1962 to 1970 and then worked as a Cardinals radio broadcaster from 1972 to 2021. This story would have been around 1984, and if this had happened ten years later, the results would have been entirely different. I had been hired for a big shoot for Anheuser-Busch. The world headquarters for the brewery was in St. Louis, and they generated a lot of work in the film/video industry. Some of their TV commercials were shot in St. Louis as well as corporate videos. The advertising agency, Darcy, Macy, MacManus, was based in St. Louis and was the agency of record for the brewery. I had worked on jobs with them for several years by this time and knew many of their art directors, producers, and client representatives.

This particular shoot was relatively large. We were shooting in a warehouse in downtown St. Louis, and I was there to make up **Jack Buck**, known for announcing the baseball games, and Mike Shannon. Jack Buck was not a friendly man. I had made him up before and knew he did not like having to do on-camera work, and was complaining about having to be there. As Anheuser-Busch owned the Cardinals baseball team, there were times that it was not a matter of choice, and this was one of those. He sat in the Winnebago, drinking coffee, and wanted to be left alone.

I was on the set, and Mike Shannon was in front of the camera working. Part of my job was to always pay attention to the talent and touch them up between takes if necessary. Mike had started to sweat, and between the prior shot and the next shot, I went out to his position, in front of the camera, to wipe the sweat and powder him so he would not be shiny. As I was standing in front of him, he reached forward with his hand and touched my breasts. He looked at me and said, "I touched your titties." I was stunned and extremely angry, but in no position where I could do or say anything. I just looked at him, and if looks could kill . . . he was a dead man, and he knew it. As I said, this was a big shoot, and it was at a time before the changes in the way men are allowed and expected to treat women had happened. As I walked back to my spot, the audio man looked at me and said, "I am sorry." I looked at the audio man quizzically, and he touched his earphones. Shannon was mic'd for his speaking part, and the audio man definitely heard what he said to me. There were fifty to sixty people on the set, and while no one saw what happened, as my back was facing all of them, the news of what happened spread amongst this large group of people. I walked off the set and stayed in my position, next to the cameraman, but I never went back to touch him up again, and no one said a word to me about it. The director never asked me to touch him up. The cameraman never asked me to touch him up. He had been drinking all day, which was not unusual behavior for him, but there are no excuses for unacceptable behavior. Times have greatly changed since this episode, and sexual harassment is no longer acceptable behavior. Had this happened today, I would have sued him and been highly successful.

POLITICS

I worked with many politicians over the years. The busiest time was during election season when the nominees were busy filming their TV commercials. Usually, they were nice and professional. My contact with them was not as friendly as with professional performers, and they were often surrounded by a variety of staff.

During the St. Louis mayoral election in the early 1980s, I had been hired by the local ABC affiliate to make up the two mayoral candidates for the city of St. Louis and the moderator for a debate. While I was busy making up one of them, I was approached by a staff member for the other candidate. I was asked to make the candidate I was making up not look good on camera. The story of Richard Nixon losing a debate against John F. Kennedy because he looked poorly on camera was well known, and I was being asked to be a part of the same form of scheme. I was polite, walked away, and made sure I made them both look as good as possible.

RICHARD 'DICK' GEPHARDT

Dick Gephardt was busy in the House of Representatives during the 1980s. There had even been talk that he might mount a presidential campaign. Mr. Gephardt had extremely reddish-blond eyebrows that one could barely see. Eyebrows set the frame for one's face, but on camera, the color made him look as if he did not have eyebrows. The first time I made him up I was penciling in his eyebrows when one of his handlers came to speak with him and then voiced his concern about what I was doing. I said, "Trust me." I explained the situation and asked this person to wait until he saw Mr. Gephardt on the monitor when he was in front of the camera. The time came, and I went to the handler and asked his opinion. He smiled and said I had been right and thanked me. This was the first time Mr. Gephardt had been made up, and his staff was unsure of the situation. Being from St. Louis, I made him up on numerous occasions, including the many times I made him up for political commercials when he was running for re-election. I made him up for portraits that were to be used in a variety of ways, and I worked with him and his wife at other times.

TOM EGGLETON

The opportunity to work with **Tom Eggleton** happened more than once. He had been a Senator for Missouri and was the expert political commentator for the local NBC affiliate. Whenever he was going to be on camera, I would be called and asked to be at the station to make him up. On one occasion, I had my work cut out for me, as he had fallen and had a black eye I needed to cover up. He teased me and said he didn't think I would be able to make it go away, and I told him he should wait and see what I was capable of. He laughed when I was finished, and the black eye was no longer visible. He said I was a true miracle worker.

There was another time I worked with him for a promotional spot for St. Louis. It was an interview that took place in a law office that had a view of the stadium for the St. Louis Rams. The interviewer started to focus his questions on Senator Eggleton's efforts to get the Rams to come to St. Louis from Los Angeles. At one point, Senator Eggleton flew into a rage and screamed that he was so much more than helping get a football team to relocate to St. Louis. He stormed out of the room, and everyone in the room looked at each other, stunned by the tirade they had witnessed. No one knew how to proceed. After a few moments of discussion between the client, the producer, and the director, amazingly, they approached me. They had observed that I had a good working relationship with the senator, and they asked if I could go and talk with him.

I walked from the room where we were filming to the office where he had gone for refuge. I asked for permission to enter, and then he and I just sat and chatted. Because I had worked with him more than once previously, we had a pleasant, professional working relationship. I chose to talk with him openly about what had just happened. I sympathized with him regarding all the important things he had done for our country, and that it was sad they were not asking the important questions. Tom Eggleton had been the vice-presidential nominee in 1972 with George McGovern. Unfortunately, he had to step down from his nomination. Of great importance, he was a great opponent of the Vietnam War, and he wanted to know why they were not asking him about his efforts to have the Vietnam War come to an end. We chatted for almost half an hour, and when I sensed he was calmer, I asked if he thought he was ready to go back and finish. He stood up and said, "Okay," and we walked back into the office, where everyone was waiting for us.

The twenty-plus years I worked as a makeup artist allowed me to *rub shoulders* with many people. Most of the people were kind, friendly, and respectful. I knew there were some people who were not chatty and with whom I needed to be professional, do my job, and not try to be a friend. There were only a few times that I was treated less than that. I was hired to make up **August Busch, Jr.**, the CEO of Anheuser-Busch in early 1980/81. I was to report to one of the dining rooms of the Anheuser-Busch headquarters building. Mr. Busch arrived with his group of assistants, ordered his breakfast, and I was told to make him up while he was eating. It was obvious that I was not permitted to talk with him, and when he got egg on his face, where I had just applied makeup, I was to keep quiet and keep him clean. I worked with Mr. Busch for about eight years. During this time, we developed a good relationship. Eventually, I didn't like having to call him Mr. Busch. I was never told I could call him by his first name, so I started calling him Mr. B.

It became clear to me that I had developed a good relationship with him when I was working with Bob Costas at the 1982 World Series. I was sitting in the dugout, where I was able to keep an eye on Bob as he did various interviews. Suddenly, I see someone waving at me. Much to my surprise, it was Mr. B. He motioned for me to come see him, where he sat in the box seats directly behind home plate. He was sitting a few seats in from the aisle, and I worked my way towards him to say hello. He was sitting next to a gentleman and said, "Linda, this is my dad, August Busch." I extended my hand and said I was honored to meet him. The next thing out of Mr. B's mouth was, "Dad, she is my makeup artist. I look down her blouse when she does it." I was flabbergasted that he chose to speak to me in such a way, and how disrespectful he was being to me as he introduced me to his father. I am almost never at a loss for words, but this was August Busch, Jr.! It took me a moment to think about what had just happened. Mr. Busch, Sr. looked at me and said in his infamous gravelly voice, "You going to let him talk to you like that?" I could have hugged him! I put my hand on my hip and, in a sassy voice, replied, "Mr. Busch—he's your son. You talk to him!" I was happy to have had the opportunity to turn an unpleasant and embarrassing moment into something feeling a bit more comfortable.

A year or two later, my family and I were dining out as we were celebrating a birthday or anniversary when someone walked up to the table to say hello. Much to my shock, it was Mr. B. I was amazed that he chose to go out of his way to say hello and acknowledge me in this manner, and I introduced him to my family. Several months later, while eating at the same restaurant, I saw him sitting at the bar with his wife, waiting for a table. Feeling as if he had given me permission to speak with him away from our working relationship, I walked over to say hello to him and meet his wife.

AND MORE

My career as a makeup artist sometimes led me to other opportunities in the film and video industry. In 1992, I was hired to be the director's assistant to **Jack Cole** for the **Kenny Rogers** TV Christmas Special. It was filmed in Branson, MO, at the theater named for Kenny, and had **Garth Brooks**, Boyz II Men, and Trisha Yearwood. It was a five-day shoot with very early morning calls. As I did in the 1960s in New York City, I had to be glued to the director's side and take notes for all his comments during rehearsals and filming. Another part of my job was to keep a log of every scene, shot, and take numbers. As the show was being videotaped, if something went wrong during the taping, they were able to re-film that particular part. The notes are very important as the director uses them when he goes to edit the film and can direct the editor to look for certain takes of any particular scene.

I got sick with the flu while doing this job, but had no choice other than to be strong and tough out the days. I had a fever, sinus problems, and coughed a lot. We were served three meals a day at the theater as we were unable to leave the grounds. One of the mornings, at 6:30, I was sitting on the ground near the trailer that provided our breakfast, feeling sick as a dog. While sitting there, a man dressed all in black, including his hat, walked by me and said, "Good morning." I said good morning back to him, and he looked down at me and asked how I was feeling. I told him that I was sick and felt terrible. He then asked if I wanted him to get me breakfast from the trailer, and I said that I didn't feel well enough to eat. I thanked him for his thoughtfulness, and he went on his way. I assumed he was one of the many men who worked at the theater. The rehearsals started, and I was in my place next to the director. It was time for Garth Brooks to come on the stage and then . . . I gasped! The man in black that I didn't know was Garth Brooks!!! I couldn't believe it.

We worked for half that day at the theater, and then we went to Silver Dollar City to film a scene in a home at the park in which Garth played his guitar and sang in front of a fireplace. It was a lovely scene. The room was very small, and they had lit a fire in the fireplace, as this was a Christmas show. I made sure that I kept as far away from Garth as I could, as I didn't want him or anyone else to get what was making me sick. When the shoot was finished, Garth thanked everyone for working with him, and then he walked across the room to be right in front of me, looked at me and said, "I hope you feel better soon." I thought it was such a kind and thoughtful thing for him to do. Oh, a side note . . . this is when Garth and Trisha met.

The following year, Jack Cole called and asked me to come work for him on a made-for-TV film he was directing. The movie was being filmed in Nashville, and as it was a low-budget film, he didn't have money in the budget to pay for my transportation to Nashville or for a hotel room. He asked if I would make the four-hour drive to Nashville and if I could stay at his home instead of a hotel. I agreed, as he was going to pay me quite well. The movie was *Proudheart* and starred **Lorrie Morgan**, the country music singer. It was a great week other than there was an unexpected snowstorm, and the weather became very cold.

PART V.

THE REST OF THE STORY

I LAUGH AS I look back at the many jobs I have had. I say that I have had more jobs than you can shake a stick at. I grew up in a family-owned business that was similar to a discount store before the term was used. It sold many items, including canned goods, furniture, appliances, and more. When I was about eight years old, my dad started taking me with him on Saturday mornings, and I spent the days marking the prices on canned goods and stocking the shelves. As I grew older, my father taught me how to use the cash register, and I would check out our customers. Of course, I also did babysitting as a teenager. I thought it was a big deal to make seventy-five cents an hour! During the years I lived in New York, I worked for a brief while at Bloomingdale's as a salesgirl in the lingerie department. I have already talked about being a ticket seller at a movie theater and working in the men's clothing company industry. I worked briefly for a travel agent who hired me after I used her to make reservations for my first trip to Europe.

After moving to St. Louis and before opening the hair salon, I worked as the assistant for a buyer for Venture Stores, which is no longer in business. They were competitors to Target. I talked about writing for *St. Louis Magazine* and my years as a makeup artist. I eventually got my real estate license and worked as a realtor for fifteen years, as I could do that and do makeup at the same time.

In 1987, I broke my rule about dating men with whom I worked. I worked off and on with my husband for six-and-a-half years before we started to date. In 1991, after living together for four years, he was in a life-threatening car fire. As he says, this was the worst day of our lives, but it turned out to be the best day of our lives. He was in a life-threatening condition for sixteen days before the doctor let me know he had crossed a bridge and that he would come home. During the next three years, he had fourteen surgeries. He was burned from head to toe, with the worst of it being from his neck up. Fortunately, he looks amazing, and with the burn more than thirty years ago, many people don't see his scars and are surprised if we mention it.

I mentioned the non-profit I worked for earlier in my story. Because of my husband's burn, we became involved with running a support group for burn survivors. This then led to working for the non-profit, which changed our lives in many ways. We spoke at national burn conferences, I wrote grants for the organization, we developed burn education programs, and I founded a camp for burn-injured children.

ONE LAST STORY

MICHAEL CHABON

Yes, I have one more *rubbing shoulders* story to tell, and this seemed to be the right place to put it. **Michael Chabon**, a bestselling author and Pulitzer Prize winner, is my favorite author. He was on a book tour promoting *Telegraph Avenue* and was appearing at a library near where I lived in St. Louis. I had already purchased the book and took it with me. After his talk, he was selling his books, as authors do. I had the book that I bought, and he autographed it for me, but I saw that he had written a children's picture book, *The Astonishing Secret of Awesome Man*, and I purchased it

Rubbing Shoulders

there. While he was signing my books, I told him about the camp I had started, and he was very interested in knowing about it and took the time to ask me questions about it. Sometime later, after I read the children's picture book, I thought it was perfect for the children who attended my camp. I called his publisher, explained that I hoped they would give me books for the children at my camp, and they said this was not an option. I then tracked down his agent's name and sent a letter to the agent explaining what I was looking for. I heard nothing back. Some time passed, and one day I received a phone call at work from a young woman asking for me. She explained that she was Michael Chabon's assistant, that they had received the letter I had sent to his agent, and that Michael had directed her to call me. I told her that I was looking for about seventy-five books to give to our campers. She asked for our mailing address, and I hoped that she would send me some books. A week or so later, this kind and generous author sent me one hundred books, enabling me to give one to each of the children who attended our camp that summer, and I had enough to give one to the counselors as well.

The years have moved on. My life has changed in many ways. My husband and I moved from St. Louis to Florida, where we are enjoying our retirement. I do not miss the cold and snow. I no longer have the experience of *rubbing shoulders* with people who are famous in one way or another, but I certainly have my memories. I look back on those years with a smile and fond thoughts.

I retired when I was seventy, and I started to learn how to paint in watercolor four years later, when I was seventy-four. Then, by accident, I wrote and illustrated a children's picture book. I have now written/illustrated two books. I go to schools to read my books to children and sell the books at markets, shops, and other events. I am always stunned when children see me somewhere and tell me they remember me reading one or both of my books at their school. When I ask what school they attend, they are always surprised when I look at them and say, "I remember that.

Linda Hansen

I was there two years ago." I never dreamed that I had the ability to have such an effect on a child. It is with great irony that I am now, in their eyes, a person those children think of as *rubbing shoulders* with. I am a firm believer that we are never too young or too old to start something new. Success is subjective; it is not objective. There is only one failure, and that is not starting to try something you want to do. I never thought or dreamed of starting another career this late in my life, but . . . here I am.

Linda Hansen

UNLIKE MANY AUTHORS, Linda Hansen never considered writing a book until a friend encouraged her to write a children's picture book. One year later, Linda was a successful author and illustrator of two creative children's books.

In 1999, in a casual discussion, Linda recounted the time she met a jazz musician. Similar conversations continued over the years, and an acquaintance finally said, "You should write a book." Multiple people offered the same suggestion, and *Rubbing Shoulders* came to be.

Linda grew up in St. Louis, Missouri, and currently lives in Florida with her husband and their dog. After retiring from her career as a non-profit executive director, she finally found the time to follow her creative passions. She enjoys expressing her love of art and nature in her watercolor paintings. In addition to writing, she speaks on "You are Never Too Young, or Too Old." Linda is proof that there is always time to start a new journey.

Visit her website for more information on Linda's books and artwork.
www.lindahansenauthor.com

SCAN HERE

www.ingramcontent.com/pod-product-compliance
Lightning Source LLC
LaVergne TN
LVHW051219070526
838200LV00064B/4967